Prophetic Covenants

Pamela Vinnett

Prophetic Covenants
Copyright © 2023 by Pamela Vinnett

First published in 2003 by Vincom Publishing Co.

ISBN 0-927936-52-6
ISBN 978-0-927936-52-1

Pamela Vinnett
P. O. Box 702160
Tulsa, Oklahoma 74170

Published by:
Joseph's Ministry, LLC
www.josephsministryllc.com

Unless otherwise indicated, all Scripture quotations are taken from The New King James Version of the Bible. Copyright © 1979, 1980, 1982, Thomas Nelson, Inc., Publishers.

All Scripture quotations marked KJV are taken from the King James Version of the Bible, electronic database. Copyright © 1988 by Biblesoft.

The Scripture quotation marked NIV is taken from The Holy Bible: New International Version. Copyright © 1973, 1978, 1984 by The International Bible Society. Used by permission of Zondervan Bible Publishers.

The Scripture quotations marked NAS are taken from the New American Standard Bible. Copyright © 1960, 1962, 1963, 1968, 1971, 1972, 1973, 1975, 1977, 1995 by The Lockman Foundation, Ha Habra, California.

Printed in the United States of America. All rights reserved under International Copyright Law. Contents and/or cover may not be reproduced in whole or in part in any form without the express written consent of the Publisher.

Contents

Introduction …………………………………………………………..3

Preface……………………………………………………………...8

Chapter 1 Why the Need for Covenant…………………………...11

Chapter 2 Fallen Angels, Fallen Man……………………………..21

Chapter 3 The Truth About Eden…………………………………27

Chapter 4 The Covenant of Man…………………………………33

Chapter 5 The Covenant of the Fathers…………………………...41

Chapter 6 God's View of Fatherhood…………………………….53

Chapter 7 The Covenant of the Woman…………………………..61

Chapter 8 Women as Ministers……………………………………71

Chapter 9 The Covenants of Abraham and Noah…………………85

Chapter 10 The Covenant of Moses………………………………95

Chapter 11 The Covenant of David……………………………...109

Chapter 12 An Ancient Blood Covenant………………………...121

Chapter 13 The Covenant of Christ……………………………...129

Chapter 14 The Melchizedek Priesthood and The Covenant of Atonement………………………………………………………141

Chapter 15 The Genealogy of Christ…………………………….151

About the Author………………………………………………...158

Introduction

From the beginning of mankind there has always been, with each developing society, a form of covenant. Though the dictionary defines "covenant" as an agreement between two parties, the scriptural definition and designation of "covenant" far exceeds this rudimentary definition. Throughout natural history we see the lines of demarcation drawn by covenants of all kinds fostering wars, marriages, executions, as well as birthing businesses, children, religions, cities and nations – the list is endless! Understanding our covenant in Christ is critical to our salvation. It is the key to our redemption and the reason for His passion.

To be ignorant of your covenant with God is to literally forfeit all of your Kingdom rights, giving them in ignorance to your enemy. This would be a travesty. A minister once told the story of a precious, illiterate black woman who worked for years for a very powerful, wealthy white man. The gentleman had family but they had no true relationship with him. In fact, his children held him in contempt. The gentleman always treated his maidservant with great respect, encouraging her to learn to read and write, if need be at his expense.

Though the woman was grateful, she thought so little of herself that she never heeded the counsel. After all, education was not a necessity for a simple little washwoman such as she. How well educated did one need to be to scrub and clean? The employer would always give the little lady some cash as payment, and a sweet little note which the woman promptly used to paper her walls in her cold, impoverished home.

Years passed and the man died. The little lady was sighted in the will, and was given by the attorneys a handsome bundle of papers. Perfect, she thought, for that last little area of the wall so desperately in need of papering. More time passed and the lonely little lady, grieved from having no purpose, passed away silently, alone, destitute and brokenhearted. When the law officers were summoned to her little hovel to claim the body for state burial, much to their utter amazement, they found the sum of one million dollars in checks and bonds, neatly pasted to the walls of the woman's despicable tomb she called home!

Needless to say, ignorance of our covenant rights is of a high consequence, just as illiteracy caused a wealthy woman to live in abject poverty. But there is a greater truth to this story that cries out to us, and that is of self-devaluation, whether fostered by our own self-hatred, or perhaps from past abuse. It is a tragic excuse for missing our Savior's great provision for our total deliverance through His death and resurrection. However, if we are not willing to study the text, His Last Will and Testament (the Bible), we will never find the fact that we are wealthy by His provision, and we will die of spiritual poverty much like the little maid died of physical poverty. Sad to say, the Bible decorates many lovely living-room tables just like the woman's decorative, high-priced wallpaper, while the inhabitants of the house languish because of the lack of the knowledge contained within its pages.

I have written this book to stir the Body of Christ to explore the many rights and privileges assigned to them by Jesus as our covenant rights in His name. Our covenant is in itself prophetic because it speaks in advance of our success if we walk in obedience to it. That notwithstanding, I never cease to be amazed by the fact that each time I have the distinct privilege of addressing any segment of the Body of Christ, I find such blatant, self-inflicted, and yes, self-indulgent, ignorance of the covenant.

The Covenant of the Prophet

Prophets and apostles enjoy a peculiar covenant with God. We are God's choice of communicating with humanity because mankind finds it much easier to receive His voice through the mouth of another human rather than an inanimate object or animal. Exodus 20:18-19 is a wonderful example of this. "Now all the people witnessed the thunderings, the lightning flashes, the sound of the trumpet, and the mountain smoking; and when the people saw it, they trembled and stood afar off. Then they said to Moses, 'You speak with us, and we will hear; but let not God speak with us, lest we die.'"

In Ephesians 2:20-22, the Apostle Paul states: "Having been built on the foundation of the apostles and prophets, Jesus Christ Himself being the chief cornerstone, in whom the whole building, being fitted together, grows into a holy temple in the Lord, in whom you also are being built together for a dwelling place of God in the Spirit." This passage and others clearly substantiate the ministries of the apostle and prophet as being the doctrine setters, foundational governmental gifts, "spiritual shepherds" and master architects to the Body of Christ. They are the two highest officers and definitively validate the existence of an actual Kingdom, and one that is godly. These power officers interpret the laws of God to the generation while illuminating the true statute of His Word.

Without the apostle and the prophet functioning in the church, the house of God fails in true biblical, scriptural and doctrinal interpretation, exposure of heresy, the inauguration of ministerial foundations, the correct institution and understanding of hierarchy in leadership, the identification and training of its officers, true discipleship, discernment of the times and seasons, ordinations, discipline, coordination of effort (the list is too extensive) and ultimately total fulfillment of generational purpose. Simply stated, to deny these officers their rightful position is as dangerous as permitting a plumber with no electrical training to wire your new home. If you would not enjoy an electrifying experience when using the commode, it is not a sensible suggestion!

Amos's declaration in chapter 3, verse 7, that "Surely the Lord GOD does nothing, unless He reveals His secret to His servants the prophets" is not just an en vogue catch phrase that has transcended the generations. It is a statement of fact – deified fact! However, the problem with it through the ages has always been the same: People invariably have a difficult time believing that the Lord God Almighty would invest that much power and authority in any mere mortal beings. This does not diminish the fact (particularly in His own sight) that He has and will continue to invest it. During seasons when the people have permitted these ministries to flourish, God has accomplished monumental feats by and through man. But, when these ministries are staunched, the effects are staggering, displaying everything from a historical declaration of the Dark Ages, to anarchy and despotism.

The church of the 21St Century must address the issue of restoration and acceptance of these last officers or else face the dismal consequences of ineffectiveness, public disassociation and abandonment. Without this vital covenant in place, we will not have a full view of defeating the terrorist efforts of Satan that fuel the terrorist efforts of men. People will escape the entrapments of what they view as the Christian religious ideology altogether and enjoy dalliance (flirting) with both world religions and witchcraft in its highest forms. It will speed us toward the end with far greater casualties than are necessary. But, because God will not ever permit the total neglect of the influence of these officers, we will still find ourselves doing the will of the One true and living God whether we believe in Him or not. He has never placed His nais-sance (founding or establishment) of covenant to a populous vote and never will. He will continue to speak it through the mouths of His prophets until the end of time as we know it, whether we acknowledge His voice or not. For a more thorough understanding of the prophet's ministry I strongly suggest that you read my book, This Psychic Prophetic Age.)

This document has been prepared from the necessary perspective of understanding covenant through the eyes of the prophetic, exploring some of the most critical covenants of our Father's Kingdom. Hopefully, these pages will enhance your understanding of biblical covenants from God's and the prophet's points of view. Though it is not my intention in this or any of my writings to appear to be an exclusive voice on the subject, it is my intention to perhaps show you a view of covenant that you probably never considered.

My prayer is that each of us, after thoroughly digging into the mysteries and uncovering the truths of the subject, might be drawn all the closer to our Savior and Lord, Jesus Christ, identifying with His passion and supreme sacrifice, while basking in the knowledge of our Kingdom rights, this time with greater wisdom and understanding.

Preface

In the vast scheme of life itself, man thrives upon answers to the unknown, and in our search for answers to the most probing questions in life, our need to know and bond with our Creator is imperative. There is no lasting relationship with God void of covenant, and each godly covenant demands a surety first from Heaven and then earth's response.

I realize that as a Bible scholar there are far too many covenants found throughout the Scriptures to explore in this particular book. Therefore, those that are deemed among the most essential will be examined from a prophetic perspective. Since all things prophetic elicit a supernatural response, the Father requires us to search out the covenants and make them a part of our life purpose.

In the 21" Century and beyond, I have prophetically given the warning found in Second Timothy 3:1-5: "But know this, that in the last days perilous times will come: For men will be lovers of themselves, lovers of money, boasters, proud, blasphemers, disobedient to parents, unthankful, unholy, unloving, unforgiving, slanderers, without self-control, brutal, despisers of good, traitors, headstrong, haughty, lovers of pleasure rather than lovers of God, having a form of godliness but denying its power: And from such people turn away!"

This profoundly cries aloud to us that in the end times it will become increasingly more difficult for us to give an accounting of what we believe. Academians will extol the virtues of historical data over wisdom of the Spirit in an attempt to cancel the validity of the Word of God and all supernatural portent. New Age gurus will espouse end-time messages riddled with the deification of man and the demotion from the deity of Christ. The question will be asked repeatedly: Can we trust the Word of God that was written by such imperfect men of questionable abilities? If the history of the Word were commonly known, would we believe what has appeared on paper for centuries? Our answer should be a resounding yes, particularly if we permit the Lord to be the interpreter of His Word and ourselves to be filled with His Spirit to receive the proper interpretation.

Therefore, we must become students of the Bible for ourselves and rely on the Holy Spirit to divulge to us its timeless truths. I believe that God foreknew this kind of problem would occur and already made provision for us. It is, however, up to you to formulate your acceptance or rejection of God's holy Word. As His agent, I desire to assist you in this quest. This is the most critical reason to write.

Chapter 1

Why the Need for Covenant

"And God said: This is the sign of the covenant which I make between Me and you, and every living creature that is with you, for perpetual generations." Genesis 9:12

One of the most remarkable attributes of our Lord is His unfailing love and His determination to keep covenant. Jehovah was, is and ever will be a covenant-keeping God. Covenant agreements throughout all of history were normally certified, approved and sealed with a written or sworn oath, document, and/or the shedding of blood. The blood covenant was the most rigid and binding, not just because it required bloodshed, but also because its stipulations warranted an oath of death to the party who breached the contract. Due to the serious nature of this agreement, the blood would be either that of a valued animal or even of a human. In studying the book of Genesis, we see the origin of all living things being in Jehovah. A careful study of the Genesis account of creation in light of the supporting scriptures gives us a wonderful assessment as to why God created mankind: for fellowship, love, adoration and glory. Humans fulfilled God's need for offspring.

There are other creatures in His sphere that were also created for fellowship and service of another kind. Job 1:6 gives us the undisputable understanding that the angels were the first to be considered "sons of God." The Hebrew inference here is derived from the word *ben* [bāne], which means son ("of a family"). The more figurative meaning of "Anointed One or in [close] relationship" is generally applied. To some scholars God as the Father of angels merely represents the originator and not the relative of the same. Therefore, it has been commonly taught that the more figurative meaning is most applicable, and that God Almighty never even implied that He had the kind of relationship with angels only shared by true fathers and sons.

However, from an intense study of the Word, we can surmise that this is exactly what the relationship was. Both Job 1:6 and Genesis 6:2 express God's view of His angelic creation. These references stand for angels and not men, and in both instances, refer to Satan himself and fallen angels as well as godly angels. Genesis says everything God made was "very good" in Genesis 1:31. Why would He create these creatures and call them very good without also including within them His very attributes? A further study shows us that God's initial intention for creating sons was fellowship and communion. Every creation of His was a direct outcome of His intense love. The one problem with angels, however, was Satan's rebellion. These marvelous creatures were unredeemable because they could not possess the one Godlike quality that would make them redeemable - a living soul.

"And the Lord God formed man of the dust of the ground, and breathed into his nostrils the breath of life; and man became a living soul" (Genesis 2:7 KJV). In this context we will examine the words "living soul." The Hebrew word for living is chay, which means to live forever (or the seed of life eternal), to be quickened, and livelihood, among other things. It comes from the word *chayah*, which means to quicken, to enliven. The Hebrew word *nephesh* is used for the word "soul" or "being." It can also be translated as the soul by which the body lives. Here *nephesh* apparently means breath. It is worthy to note that the same word used in Numbers 16:30 expresses that it can be killed, and in Numbers 31:19 it can be poured out with the blood. The passionate existence of a person is its meaning in Leviticus 17:11, which says that life is in the blood.

When the body dies it is separated from the soul. The spirit and soul are swept swiftly into their interminable destiny. God disdains necromancers, spiritists and mediums because they often peer into the realms of hell and see the damned who are suspended there. They are enabled to do so by the covenant they have made with the unremitting realms of darkness. Those who are of hell's kingdom can assuredly gaze into her bedchambers.

Hell is a void in the spirit realm created for Satan and those who follow his demands. It is horrid and unthinkably ominous, for its true definition is *separation from God*! This is the paramount argument for the preaching of the gospel and an understanding of covenant. Simply put, we preach to the masses so that everyone can receive an opportunity to miss the second death that is hell. We teach the truth about God's covenant so as to assure its partners the liberties and comfort this covenant affords, including not living a hell on earth and then being consigned to one for all eternity.

When the soul lives as though in Heaven on earth, it will live in Heaven with God evermore, for God blesses those who keep His covenant. This is good news. A conclusion must be drawn from these varying definitions that explains the true meaning of living soul, and that is that man's spirit is actually a "quickening" soul, or a soul which is alive and also can bring to life one like it. The concept here is man as a spirit being lives in a body that is intertwined with his mind, which is often synonymous with his heart (soul). The mind, body and spirit are so tightly woven together that only God by His Word can divide them (Hebrews 4:12). There is actually little to no inference in the Scripture that even implies that man should make an issue of dividing these entities. It should be sufficient enough for us to know we have them.

Also we must consider the fact that if we eat poison in the form of certain foods, or take in pollutants from the air by accident, it does not just adversely affect the body but the mind and spirit also. That is why we must stand on our covenant rights that if we drink (take in) any deadly thing by accident, through ignorance, or by the plan of our enemy, it will not harm us. However, if we deliberately take in deadly things, whether through poor diet, pornographic books or movies, or even verbal harassment, anything given by us or directed toward us can potentially harm us!

The Bible says it is *"not what goes into the mouth [that] defiles a man; but what comes out of the mouth, this defiles a man"* (Matthew 15:11). We must carefully consider then that whatever defiles us defiles us, *mind, body* and *spirit*. An unpolluted spirit gives birth to healthy, sane spirits in the humans we both create and associate with. It causes us to have a fuller understanding of the *chayah* principle in God's Kingdom.

This quickening spirit has the ability to be *recreated*, or better stated, *procreated*, through the reproduction of mankind in the womb. In other words, man sires a child and the child is given a living soul from its conception, and thus will be born with a soul intact. This factor singularly relegates abortion to being tantamount to murder (especially when performed as a result of lasciviousness) for the Christian believer, seeing that **the human soul is in the blood of the male**, as will be discussed later. Likewise, the value and power of blood are dramatically revealed through this extraordinary disclosure which precisely explains why Adam's sin brought bloodguilt to all humanity and the pollution of every human soul. The souls of his posterity were in his loins at the time sin entered. It is no longer necessary for God Almighty to breathe the breath of life into anyone born legally from the womb, for He did it in the first Adam and the ability remained. This is a part of God's covenant with mankind.

Angels are purely spirit beings who are alive, but cannot reproduce as spirit alone. Therefore, they are not "quickening" souls and once terminated, can never be brought back to life by any means other than possession of a body. Death spoken of in this context means to be separated from the life that is of God for all eternity and not virtual nonexistence. Further, angels lack that most important part of God that raises mankind to "God-likeness" status: a female counterpart with procreative abilities, and a male with seed with which to impregnate. We will examine this further later in the text. Scripture gives us the key to this fact. Hebrews 1:5,13 poses the question to us, *"For to which of the angels did He ever say: 'You are My Son, today I have begotten You'? And again: 'I will be to Him a Father, and He shall be to Me a Son'? ... 'Sit at My right hand, till I make Your enemies Your footstool'?"*

The startling truth of the matter is angels do not possess the part of God's sonship that could put them in the class of man called [exact] "likeness and image.' When God created man He made him in His exact likeness and image, and man became a living soul. Not just a living being to praise, commune, think and fellowship, but an eternal being who feels, loves, despises, honors, creates, and yes, even procreates like his Maker.

It was further decreed by the Creator that God's Son, the Lord Jesus, would become the firstborn of many brethren. Fallen angels could not supply an equivalent to be born a spirit, and by so doing, redeem angels. There can be no angelic equivalent of Christ. There is no sacrifice to make of a seedless spirit being, and just as cru-cial, no **blood** which carries within it a certain life-giving characteristic with which to appease the King of Heaven or any god for that matter. Angels cannot create or procreate by their own matter, and thus the sacrifice of one does not bear out quite the same. However, their failure caused excruciating pain to the heart of the Father.

The Lord considers the death of one of His own as precious according to the Psalms. How could the death of an angel, who has no understanding of the value of *giving* life for life, be exactly the same to God, and how could the death of a seedless, bloodless spirit bring deliverance to their kind? The Word of God says the angels cannot comprehend the song of deliverance or salvation. It is impossible for them to be saved, making salvation only vicariously comprehensible to them. This lends new meaning to Genesis 1:6.

Further, it is necessary that mankind have the ability to procreate so that each successive generation presents the possibility of bringing forth children who become better and closer to God. The sins of the fathers are visited upon the children to the fourth generation, however the blessing of the righteous to one thousand generations.

Exponentially, the possibility of a more godly generation exists in this scriptural fact than an ungodly. Thusly, a creature of His own creation simply will not get the best of God. Since this is true, it is quite preposterous in my estimation to present Satan as being great or too highly influential toward the overthrow of the Kingdom of God, the Church or Heaven. He must be presented as unequal in every way to the Almighty and totally capable of defeat in the sight of God by the Father first and second by His equipped, assigned agents. No scriptural account acknowledges how or when the angels were created, but only by whom. And, no scripture states that they were made as vulnerable or equal to mankind. The Psalms express that man is made a little lower than the "Elohim," angelic beings, lords and rulers of the heavens; the heavenly hosts (Psalm 8:5).

Some believe this should be translated God-exclusively (in times past I taught the same), and not include in the definition the heavenly host. However, other uses of the word more than imply that the heavenly host should be included in the definition in this context. Second Peter 2:11 speaks of angels as being greater in power and might. This, along with other scriptures, provides a basis for this sensible conjecture. An argument ensuing throughout the Body of Christ insists that man has been given by his Creator authority to command angels. There has not been given any specificity to this extraordinary claim by anyone purporting the revelation that I have found to be sound. An honest examination of the Word firmly concludes this cannot be possible. The scripture just alluded to in Second Peter discloses to us the thought that angels hold astonishing abil-ities. Though the Greek word for "angel" does not give us as well-defined an understanding of the power and authority given these magnificent creatures, the Hebrew definition of two words for angels does quite superbly.

One Hebrew word for "angel" found interspersed throughout the Old Testament is sar, meaning a prince, a ruler, a leader, a chief, a chieftain, an official, a captain; a vassal, a noble, an official (under a king), a general, a commander (military), a head, an overseer (used of other official classes), heads, princes (used of a religious office). The list is quite inclusive according to *The Brown, Driver and Briggs Hebrew Lexicon*.[1] Another Hebrew word for angel, mal'ak, gives a greater context to their power: to dispatch as a deputy, messenger, possessor whose message covers impartation, dispensation, revelation and rulership. How have we concluded then that God would place them under our authority and control, much less our whims? If Christians in general were so graced with such a privilege, the Lord would surely make it plainer in His text. It would also have to be discovered whether some or all of these magnificent beings were to be so controlled for they have differing authorities according to rank and delegation from the Father. The supposition is generally based upon one scripture in particular found in Hebrews 1:14 that aptly presents the fact that angels are ministering spirits sent to minister to the heirs of salvation. We must theologically conclude that God is the sender. The verse merely clarifies why and to whom they are sent.

If the truth were known, the greater measure of humanity has met with grave difficulty attempting to command other men. Our ability to judge what should or should not be demanded or requested of angels should be based upon our maturity. Reality dictates it is unfathomable what disasters could be incurred through reckless, irresponsible, immature creatures commanding God's holy power creation. If His Word speaks of our not knowing "how to pray as we

---

[1] The Online Bible, Thayer's Greek Lexicon and Brown, Driver & Briggs Hebrew Lexicon (Canada, Ontario: Woodside Bible Fellowship, 1993).

ought," why should we be endowed with such directives? The Almighty simply would not be so ludicrous as to permit mankind to indiscriminately enjoy such unsubstantiated power for angels to be at the beck and call of most of us regardless of our spirituality. I have even observed precious ones inflated with egotistical misunderstanding and misguided importance, assuming they could command the great archangels Michael and Gabriel, yet these beloved ones have no great command over their own fleshly appetites or pious obedience.

The sum of the matter is, these amazing creatures are God's possession *sent* to us, and they are exclusively under His command. We must request the Father commission them to be properly submitted to the premise of His Kingdom. They are not ours to command of our own volition. Angels simply do not respond to our command because they do not take orders from our words, but God's. Because of this, we must realize that *angels will only respond to the Word of God being spoken by us in the earth.*

First Corinthians 6:3 says, *"Do you not know that we shall judge angels?"* The Apostle Paul's declaration would seem to imply that the more generic terminology applies to the word "angel," but this of course is erroneous. The phrase, "we shall judge.," in the Greek uses *krino*, which means properly, to distinguish, i.e., decide (mentally or judicially); by implication, to try, condemn, punish: In the King James Version of the Bible – avenge, conclude, condemn, damn, decree, determine, esteem, judge, go to (sue at the) law, ordain, call in question, sentence to, think.[2] This expansive definition well delineates the context in which the impressive apostle writes. He is wholly relegating the instruction to fallen angels and not holy angels. There is no reason for the mortal to judge the immortal righteous.
Man did not begin as a "little lower than Elohim." He began in an estate that was higher than the angelic hosts. Jehovah's judgment *after*

---

[2] The New Exhaustive Strong's Numbers and Concordance with Expanded Greek-Hebrew Dictionary (Biblesoft and International Bible Translators, Inc., 1994).

the fall relegated him to the estate now occupied that will be restored to him after the restoration of all things in the Millennial Kingdom and beyond.

Man was created from the dust of the earth to dwell in the earth. But it was not until the Lord breathed into him the breath of life that his mortal frame took on life. His ability to take on or retain eternal life was strictly based upon obedience to the command of the Father.

Chapter 2
Fallen Angels, Fallen Man

From a prophetic perspective, the stage was set in the Garden of Eden for mankind to inherit the greatest gift of all from God, eternal life. Two trees became the focus of attention in the midst of the garden. To obey meant to freely eat of the tree of life; disobedience dictated to eat of the tree of the knowledge of good and evil. All that was necessary was for them to consider the teachings rendered to Adam by the Ancient of Days and simply obey them.

Instead, on the strength of the word of the serpent, Satan, all of God's benefits were forfeited, causing God to put in motion the plan of redemption for His prized possession. Satan had won a victory that would prove to be the torment of all mankind from that moment on. What caused this yielding to Satan's seduction to have such weight? The answer is found in Ezekiel 28 and Isaiah 14.

"You were the seal of perfection, full of wisdom and perfect in beauty. You were in Eden, the garden of God. ... You were the anointed cherub who covers; I established you.. You were perfect in your ways from the day you were created, till iniquity was found in you. By the abundance of your trading you became filled with violence within, and you sinned; therefore I cast you as a profane thing out of the mountain of God; and I destroyed you, O covering cherub…" Ezekiel 28:12-16

"How are you fallen from heaven, O Lucifer, son of the morning! How you are cut down to the ground, you who weakened the nations! For you have said in your heart: 'I will ascend into heaven, I will exalt my throne above the stars of God; I will also sit on the mount of the congregation on the farthest sides of the

north; I will ascend above the heights of the clouds, I will be like the Most High.' Yet you shall be brought down to Sheol, to the lowest depths of the Pit." Isaiah 14:12-15

Both Ezekiel and Isaiah paint a vivid picture of Satan's fall from Heaven and from grace. The scripture says he was perfect until iniquity was "found" in him, but who found it? The dissident himself! This abhorrent celestial spirit reputed that he could by some inconceivable means take dominion over the heavens and the earth, exalting his sovereignty above the Most High.

Likewise, God's laws apply to all creation and are contingent upon strict obedience. Satan was given a great amount of authority. Ezekiel makes the statement, *"You were in Eden, the garden of God."* The prophet further deliberates, *"You were the anointed cherub who covers."* Can this be an implication of Satan's assigned territory in his kingdom on *earth*? Some Bible scholars believe this to be more than an implication, thus explaining why this fallen angel could be given carte blanche to persuade and finally seduce mankind, taking control of their lives and ascertaining a form of lordship (becoming a god or lord) in their Kingdom.

The hypothesis concludes that he was merely attempting to take back a sphere of domain from which he was deposed. Perhaps the mention of "covering" is pertaining to the creatures that God would place in the Garden of Eden. After being cast out of the mountain of God, this foe set himself in position to endeavor to displace and eliminate the authority of the Father in the earth and ultimately in Heaven (the initial plan).

Numerous Bible teachers point to the instruments spoken of in Ezekiel 28:13 KJV as being embedded in his body, but the scripture does not really say or even imply this is a correct interpretation. It is better stated in subsequent translations as being created for him in the day that he was created. This misinterpretation has led some to believe that Satan somehow was the praise and worship leader of Heaven. He simply was not. He was called the anointed cherub who covers, who was permitted to walk among the fiery stones (serpentine-like angels) of Heaven. Being cherubim and not seraphim denotes God's ranking system placed cherubim as being possibly a little lower in authority than the seraphim or the archangels. Satan was not classified with the seraphs but walked in the holy mountain of God with them by assignment and God's favor.

There were other angels that fell prey to his deception, but were not permitted to contiguously manifest on earth. Their powers were understandably too great. Therefore Jehovah reserves them in the chains of hell until an appointed time. Revelation 9:11 cites a powerful and wicked angel (actually a conglomeration of fallen angelic powers) as the king of the abyss (bottomless pit). In the Hebrew, his name is Abaddon. In the Greek, it is Apollyon. Abaddon stems from the Hebrew word *abad*, which means to annihilate and destroy. These fallen spirits hold greater power than Satan and will be released for a short time in the midst of the Tribulation.

Even though Satan has been erroneously classified as being higher and greater in authority than all of the other angels, few deal with the aspect of his trafficking or trading. God demands fairness and equity in the commerce of His Kingdom. It is a necessity to distribute the beneficial aspects of His goodness to the nations. How much more so would this demand be an absolute law in Heaven to be strictly obeyed by His created servants? An unjust weight or balance in Jehovah's economy is an abomination He abhors. Apparently, Lucifer committed this fraudulence in the sight of God openly as if he were privileged. By his great "trading" he became proud and increased in wealth (the lord of foolish mammon). His ego beleaguered his senses, and a spirit monster was born. As a result of Lucifer observing his own beauty and authority, he actually thought to rival the Most High! This thought process alone was apparently enough to start the avalanche of corruption that cost him his place in God's eternity.

The New Testament says in John that God is a light and in Him is no variable of darkness. Therefore Satan, like man, was made from the heart of God, perfect. However, if you take what is perfect and filled with light and put it in a place where it, through rebellious thoughts and actions, can discover darkness, iniquity will be born. The closer you get to the full light of God and His pure goodness, the greater tiny spots, blemishes and sins are illuminated. This was the problem with Satan; he received darkness over light. One single act of disobedience mushroomed into full-blown decadent rebellion, for Satan was under the canopy and thus in the shadow of the Almighty. The same kind of symmetry would be displayed if a ripe, plump potato was taken from the rich soil in full bud, placed in a darkened room for many weeks and permitted to shrivel and decay. At the end of the term, this fruit of the earth would be gnarled and rotting, and the stench of it would almost be unbearable. So was the outcome of Satan's insurrection against God. Equally as graphic was the fall of man in Eden.

Who found the iniquity in Satan? Satan found it in thoughts and actions of rebellion. God Almighty uncovered it and permitted him to act it out to its fullest potential. Our Father had to do this or all creation would serve Elohim out of terror rather than love, godly fear and respect. As soon as his (Satan's) iniquity was fulfilled, God simply discharged him from Heaven. The Almighty never touched him by His own hand lest He destroy him utterly.

The other angels (higher in rank) who warred against him followed the dictates of the Sovereign, and Satan was dramatically discharged, along with approximately one-third of the then existing angels. Now the inhabitants of the earth were to feel his venom against the Lord! First John 5:7 reveals that God had a summit in Heaven with the Word and the Spirit, and at the proper point in eternity, the Word agreed to go. It was also at that precise moment in eternity that He became the Lamb slain, literally before and from the foundation of the earth. God set everything in motion. *Before* Satan fell, the Lamb was slain within the heart of God, and the universe was molded and shaped. Tucked within its bosom was a peculiar little planet called earth, specially made by the hands of God for the object of His affection, mankind. The earth was the bridal gift for His wife, the redeemed human being.

But, by the entrance of man, Satan had already fallen to earth, setting himself up to defile God's beauty and grandeur. Upon seeing God's creation, man, Satan determined that he would gain full possession of this enigma. Knowing the ideology surrounding the Kingdom of God, he surmised that this being would be granted extraordinary power, and if this power could be harnessed, he would once again obtain the reward of a place of dominion. In essence, he would become the god of the earth. The thinking here was logical to a spirit being, particularly one who is no longer in fellowship with the Father, vehemently angry, and still aspiring to win a victory – the same act of rebellion which caused him to lose his seat in Heaven. This cherub's plan was calculated, devious and deadly. He was already a victim of the second death from which there is no redemption. If he could, through seduction, entice the man to fail in the same manner as he himself failed, he would have a powerful access to God, and a new seat of dominion.

The aforementioned scriptures in Ezekiel and Isaiah show us Satan's plans from Heaven down and earth up. The master tempter has an extraordinary mind, and imagined himself seated literally in the place of kings in the congregation on the sides of the north. He boasted, *"I will be like the Most High"* (Isaiah 14:14). In verse 13 he said, *"I will exalt my throne above the stars of God,"* an insane, delusional thought at best. When a comparison of scriptures is done between Ezekiel 28 and Isaiah 14, along with Genesis 1:26 *("Let Us make man in Our image")*, definition is given to the phrase "I will be like the Most High," for the one created being in the universe that is proposed as being like God is man. Satan desired to be like mankind, or more specifically, to take the place of man as a spiritual entity and authority. This would be best accomplished by taking over (possessing) man.

In Genesis, chapter 6, the "sons of God" (an allusion to fallen angels) took wives of the fair daughters of men, siring children by them. These became "men of renown," mutated giants, abnormally deformed or disfigured beings. They were a frightful people who terrorized the nations round about them. What was the ultimate goal of Satan? It was two-fold: to obtain children through the womb of mankind, and to gain entrance into the bloodline of man.

Thus, such access would result (he foolishly conjectured) in coming into the bloodline of redemption! This was a plan to regain covenant with God's Kingdom, an illegally won, merciless covenant that would force Jehovah to allow him the right to ascend above the throne of the Almighty. Of course, this plan was not and could not ever be realized, for God had already made provision for the fall of man.

Chapter 3
The Truth About Eden

In my dissertation concerning Eden, I will examine it from the standpoint of one who believes in the infallibility of the truths contained within the Word of God. Whether there was a literal garden or a figurative, didactic fictional piece of land, the ideologies espoused in the story prove its necessity to the recounting of the overall human story. Scientific evidence challenges the most astute scholar to believe that this story is pure fantasy or Jewish fable. However, even if speculation and raw evidence concluded the latter view to be true, the spiritual premise upon which the story is predicated validates a divine exigency to tell it. No matter what side of the fence you may be on concerning the reality of Eden, the fact is to ignore its vital lesson will surely result in repeating it. I will deal with the entire issue throughout this book from the standpoint of a literal, vital truth being espoused to man from God. Though this view appears to point to a literal Eden, the principles will still apply to a figurative Eden, for divine standards persevere on their own whether believed or not.

There is remarkably no greater event in the continuous purpose of God to define the absolute necessity for a covenant with Jehovah than that of the cataclysmic fall of man in Eden. Satan, who had been ousted from his favorable position in Heaven, had now been hurled violently to earth and was watching with transfixed eyes to see this new creation of God he had heard of in Heaven. After perusing the situation, he determined that he would have no difficulty debunking the truths expressed to these creatures by God. Lucifer systematically pulled upon his extraordinary mental and spiritual abilities to empower him with a plan to undo Adam and Eve. It is most commonly assumed that the fall of man came as a direct result of love for a woman, but critical study of the Word of God betrays the romantic fantasy so many western Bible philosophers would love to weave into the tapestry of Eden.

Adam's failure came as a result of disobedience coupled with beguilement of his spouse and an alien's search for a womb. Adam was just as captivated as his spouse and would have fallen prey to the seduction himself if he had been the direct object of it. Sad to say, he, Adam, was the indirect object of Satan's contempt, and not the direct object. Ultimately, he would function as a sperm bank for the wicked one's use. The direct object was Eve, the "wombed male" man. Why? Eve (*Chavvah* in Hebrew) was desirable in more ways than our minds can comprehend. To a disembodied spirit she supplied more than just a body as her male counterpart could provide, and she possessed the ability to produce many others through her womb. Eve was rightly named by her husband, Adam, for indeed she was the mother of all living (human) things. Adorned with a perfect human body, she could only produce perfect human beings with living souls, brilliant minds and the ability to house more deviance than any devil could gleefully dream of handling. As a perfect and matured human, she and her husband were initially constructed greater than Satan. She was a reproducer, and in her prime would be capable of producing a master race of people profoundly spiritual and seemingly limitless in capabilities, especially in the right hands. The dragon knew that she was the one possession he must have, for as a dead, destroyed, disemboweled, bodiless spirit, he had no chance of reproducing after his own kind. It then became necessary to produce another kind; he was after a womb and a wife. Adam could supply neither and was not nearly as fine a catch as Eve in the beginning.

Women were and still are the targets. That is why they are hated or revered in every society throughout every generation. The demons of society will continue to have her worshiped or scorned so that she will turn to the dark master to become her husband, or source of power, and friend, for this master knows that she possesses the way to bring him at least four generations of children if she yields to his pleasantries. He must pervert the seed to gain life and power. The Garden of Eden represented a fertile, fully equipped land patterned after the perfection of Heaven but filled with the treasures of earth. It was a sumptuous and complete world for exploration and human enjoyment. If the temptation had been unsuccessful, mankind would have enjoyed an extraordinary and fruitful existence that would have taken an eternity to explore. The perfection that existed in their physical forms could have taken them through possible millennia without death prevailing, whether they partook of the tree of life or not.

In the midst of the Garden were two critically important trees: the tree of life and the tree of the knowledge of good and evil. The Garden's exact dimensions were not clarified purposely. God desired for it to be thought of as an enormous nation would be visualized. Therefore, the position of the trees is important, in that they were at the point of the heart of the "nation," so to speak. It is also worth mentioning that these trees were beside one another and not out of sight of each other. The type of fruit that grew upon each tree is totally immaterial. For those who have problems believing in the trees, a single garden or a talking serpent, it suffices us to know that the lesson behind the story is more important than even the symbols of the story. Whether Jehovah had offered them to drink from the cistern of life and shun the sister of good and evil, or eat of the tree of life, the lesson is still the same:

Disobedience brings death, obedience brings life. The fruit of the tree of the knowledge of good and evil could rightly be called the fruit of wicked disobedience. The fruit of the tree of life could be called communion and life. Man made the wrong choice and thus forfeited his high estate in the supernatural realm. Because of this forfeiture, man has no supernatural abilities within himself at birth, but now must appeal to a deity, true or false, to empower him in the supernatural realm.

Prior to the fall in Eden, man was given a command to eat of the tree of life. This emphatically implies to us that man did not have "eternal" life without eating of the tree of life. What does this mean? In actuality, man was mortal and needed to obtain immortality by taking in immortality through obedience. If this standard had not been set, there would be no justification for instituting communion later, for it is the taking in of the fruit of the tree of life. It is most commonly believed that the life spoken of here is applicable only to the physical body, yet it is obvious they were physically alive before and after the fall. This would not make sense if the thought process concerning it were from God's perspective. Therefore, Genesis 2:9, in speaking of the tree of life, must use the definition "everlasting life" for the word *chay*, whereas its definition in Genesis 2:7, speaking of the creation of man, is rightly translated "quickening [able to replicate] spirit or breath of life." Now we can sensibly apply the more unusual meanings of the word for soul (*nephesh*), which is defined as continuing to live by drawing breath, and an entity that can be killed if the blood is poured out, along with the strangest meaning of the word (as found in Haggai 2:13), one who has died, with emphasis on the person's identity while they yet live. Therefore, the nephesh (spirit) of Adam meant the whole person, heart, will, desire, and not the eternal person, without the fruit of the tree of life.

Scripture discloses that Jesus bought back the defiled covenant right to have eternal life and eternal purpose through the cross. He willingly became the fruit of the tree of life that we might eat of it and live everlastingly. However, Jesus' sacrifice will not buy physical interminable life until the spiritual force called death, hell and the grave is totally vanquished and perpetually destroyed in the flames of hell along with Satan as its author. If man had lived on without eating of either tree, he would have eventually perished, and the spirit would have died. This is why God commanded them to eat of the tree of life. The entire application was a precursor to the necessity and power to believe in the Word of God as perpetual and to receive the Word made flesh after their disobedience.

The second premise was much more difficult to acquire and required God coming as man to redeem mankind. If everlasting life had been given at creation alone and not through creation and obedience, the whole plan of God would be ineffective. The Holy One would not be able to take man to Himself because man would be a sinner beyond redemption; a lost, living dead spirit just like his enticer. His sin would still be a form of disobedience, for he was commanded to eat of one tree and not to eat of the other. The Word says that the wages of sin is death. This is a Kingdom prin-ciple. But, though they had earned the wage, provision was made for them before the world was framed to inherit the eternal life they had forfeited. Even the wrong tree was still a creation of God and thus carried within it a kernel bearing the promise of life, for God cannot create anything for death alone. The entrance of His Word brings life to every situation.

The seed of life was placed within Adam as a quickening spirit. Eating of the wrong tree caused separation from God. It is sensible to assume that man would have eventually eaten from one tree or the other, but everything that the Father made was geared toward the consumption of the meat of the tree that would bring life. Ask yourself this question: If God had already given eternal life and not just life and breath, why create a tree of life? And, why would Genesis 3:22-24 inform us that Jehovah drove the man and woman out of the garden because they had become as *"one of Us, to know good and evil"* (v. 22). It is because of the continuation of that verse, "Lest he put out his hand and take also of the tree of life, and eat, and live forever." Obviously, this tree's fruit had to do with a supernatural enhancement and not merely a natural one.

Once again, the New Testament clearly states that Jehovah had already made provision for the failure of humanity. This is the sole reason for the tree being the object of testing, for in the fullness of time, God Himself would come to earth to become the fruit of a tree that brings life to those who believe. Whenever we take communion, we are once again experiencing eating from the tree of life. After having made the wrong choice, Adam and Eve were forced from the Garden of God's delight, brought into bond servitude to the devil and had sentenced all mankind from that moment on to be conceived in sin and fashioned in iniquity. God had to provide a savior, for since man brought sin into the world, a man had to be sacrificed to save men from the sin of the world.

Chapter 4
The Covenant of Man

Then God said, "Let Us make man in Our image, according to Our likeness; let them have dominion..." "And the Lord God formed man of the dust of the ground, and breathed into his nostrils the breath of life; and man became a living being." Genesis 1:26, 2:7

Contrary to what the spirit world of darkness would dictate, man is not the natural enemy of woman, nor is he the enemy of God. Someone once said, speaking of male-female relationships, "Women should not be referred to as the opposite sex in relation to the male, but should be called the corresponding sex." Mankind was created to be a companion and servant to his Creator, thus becoming the extension of God's dominion and love in the earth. The relationship between God and man is parallel to the relationship between husband and wife. Eden could not divert or stop this decree from Heaven, for man's redemption by his Creator was conclusively settled in eternity before he was ever predetermined in the earth. It is comforting to know that the cumulative efforts of all the evil men and women ever born were not enough to prevent our Father from bringing us to the glorious light of salvation.

Evil cannot outdo love, its opposition. Likewise, our Heavenly Father provided a covenant plan for each individual who would receive it, and the seed of His plan was actually prophesied in Eden.

Then God said, "Let Us make man in Our image, according to Our likeness; let them have dominion..."
Then God blessed them, and said to them, "Be fruitful and multiply; fill the earth and subdue it; have dominion ...over every living thing that moves on the earth."
Genesis 1:26, 28

In verse 29 of this same chapter, God introduces to mankind the laws of seedtime and harvest. These laws were the keys to everything that would be governed by man in the prophecy contained within the preceding verses, for every living thing had to contain the seed within it for reproduction. In this law was the assurance of a "righteous seed" that would redeem forever the fallen seed. Jehovah had already, in the course of creation, made the animal and plant life that were to fall under the dominion of the male and the female, each having within it the composition of regeneration. At the conclusion of His creation, God expresses His satisfaction by saying that it was good and very good. Everything necessary to foster life and covenant now was in place. God could rest in it, setting precedence for our having a Sabbath's rest. He also in that eternal moment set the laws in motion that governed the reproductive powers of the earth, for just as the womb of the female had to rest after birth (sexual contact with the wife was relegated to being deterred until after her time of cessation of bleeding and the closing of the womb. Medical science gives this period a time of six to eight weeks), so did the earth have to rest each seventh year for revitalization.

With the fall of man came a necessity for mankind to reclaim its prophetic Kingdom rights. The laws of God were then devised, based upon regulation of the lawbreaker (whether it be human or fallen angel) as much as governmental information from the Kingdom of light. It is a worthy observation in fact that God's laws of the earth never bowed to the kingdom of darkness, nor were actually adversely affected by it. His rule remained intact. It was man who suffered and had to be given ways to subdue the false gods and their entrapments in order to open an avenue of opportunity to commune and communicate with the God of Heaven. The laws of God therefore were enacted to punish evildoers and supply an effective way for man to rule in the Kingdom created for him, now by default given over to his enemy.

We must acknowledge the fact that the Lord never changed the process of creation from the way He initially secured it before the fall, but rather changed the manner in which man would labor to achieve success within it. Due to the curse upon the ground, the earth, along with a potentially bountiful harvest, yielded thorns and thistles. Man had to sweat for his bread and fight the very elements the word of the Lord said he was to subdue. Women had increased sorrow in conception and in bringing forth their children in pain. Husbands ruled over wives, and children (still comprised of the dust of the earth after the flesh) rebelled to the point of murder.

Yet in all this, the laws of God governing seedtime and harvest never failed or changed. Like still procreated after like, kind after kind according to the seed within. If murder and rebellion were planted in the heart of any creature, it would be reproduced in the seed. Woman was told that her Seed would bruise his (the serpent's) head. Women bear no seed, but men plant seed within them. This not only stood for the Christ who was to come, but for all children born of men who would follow the ways of the Christ.

The fallen dragon of Heaven saw a perfect opportunity to be planted, resurrected and given new life through fallen man. He successfully entered the seed of the firstborn human being from the womb and set a precedent for other angelic beings to desire children by fallen humanity. We could conjecture that this was simply too enticing a temptation to resist. But in this, God proved His sovereignty, for despite Satan's possession of Cain, God possessed Abel, the next son born of the same fallen parents. The blessing of covenant with Adam could not be accomplished if all Adam's offspring were cursed by his failure. Of course, it is worthy of note to say Cain had much to do with the decision concerning possession. He chose to yield to the serpent. God proved that ***the curse was not on the humans but on the ground and on God's enemy.*** Satan was given the right to take the first child produced by fallen parents who sired him still under the throes of the intoxication of the fruit of disobedience. This factor was not the exclusive aspect that gave him access to Cain as has been presupposed. Satan's point of access was the rebellious consequence of a mind ripe and ready to sin, which was proven to be so by the sacrifice this first son rendered to *the* God of Heaven and earth.

The governor of hell could not have the next son, for he moved by the dictates of following the hidden laws of God that demanded life had to be given to atone for the sins of those things living. For any creature who feared God, the atoning sacrifice would never have contemptuously been offered as that of mere life-sustaining fruit of the ground. Rather, it would have been precluded that an offering of something that was *of* the earth but not only taken *out of* the earth would exclusively be acceptable.

What does this mean? Cain offered what could be humanly reproduced and of inferior value to that which could only reproduce by the living laws of God. Planting seed could beget more vegetation even after the death of the parents. The death of a lamb, particularly a male, destroyed the possibility of any future generations through its blood, drastically increasing its value. Nothing that could potentially spring forth into life of its own accord could atone for something that could only reproduce and have life by both a covenantal act of copulation and a divine intervention or impregnation. It was by a plant that the father and mother of mankind fell prey to its enemy. It was by the shed blood (which contains life for flesh; plants have no exact equivalent of it) of an innocent living being that proper atonement had to be made, proving that Abel's heart was after God and righteousness. Further, mankind was not carnivorous at this point. A lamb would be considered very precious. Abel became the first recognized human sacrifice that set all of Heaven in motion to bring about absolution for the sins of mankind instead of vengeance against it. Through his death, sin had taken a malevolence turn. According to ancient history, lambs were also symbolic of princes.

God was making a Statement of those things that were to come, for the Prince of Peace would die for the sins of all.

The male of the species called mankind is the singular focal point upon which all of the ascertained order of the Kingdom revolves. As was discussed in the chapter titled "Why the Need for Covenant," all spirits are male, even the ones that reside inside the bodies of the female humans in the earth. These spirit beings are referred to as "spirit man" in the generic sense, just as human beings are called mankind. It is necessary to set this premise so as to rightly interpret the covenant of the male and see the unique difference between it and the covenant of the female.

Creation and Science

The creation story seems to be preposterous to the thinking, logical human mind, particularly when we consider the exhumation of ancient human bones that show a more animal-like form of early mankind. I would like to offer a sensible theory as to how some of the scientific findings may support the Word of God in several ways. First, God does not give us a picture of what man originally looked like, leaving much to the imagination of fallen man to envision the look of antediluvian man. If it were necessary to have a clear picture of Adam and Eve that differed from the old skeletal remains presently on exhibit, God would have made another provision for it. It is sensible to think that these findings have validity and can perfectly correlate with the Judeo-Christian belief of God Jehovah being the Creator of all things. Some scientists, for example, are presupposed to believe that all life began in theory with a huge bang in outer space, and particles fell to earth and somehow evolved into all life. The argument further states that creatures spawned in the oceans evolved through necessity into another kind of creature that crawled ashore and adapted itself to its environment, thus eventually turning into man.

Though all of these speculations may bear a small thread of truth, none of them specifically answers the truth concerning the creation and/or evolution of man, and that is if there is any sanity to the theory, *where did the life that fell to earth originate*? In the most literal sense, it existed in the mind of the Spirit after which God gave it life. Scientists in modern times sent a space module equipped with cameras and computers into space for the purpose of exploring the planet Mars. Sad to say, this first piece of equipment to make it there and send back pictorial images as well as other scientific data, was lost. However, it transmitted extremely valuable information prior to its loss. One fascinating projection showed the existence of water (H_2O) on the mystery planet. This suggests that when mankind was going through the dark ages of understanding, God was still bringing clarity to all things pertaining to Him, for had science only consulted Genesis 1:6-8, it would have discovered the fact that God separated the waters, which were under the firmament from the waters above the firmament. Genesis 1:8 says that *"God called the firmament Heaven..."* All this was achieved before the time period asserted to as the close of the second day. How is "firmament" defined? According to the *Hebrew and Greek Lexicon* by Spiro Zhodiates, it is the Hebrew word *raqiya*, which means expanse, the sky, the vault of Heaven (space). Genesis 1:14, 17 points to an expanse of sky which is farther from the earth, containing the stars, the sun and the moon.

According to the Word of God, water was assuredly in the heavens, and with these findings we can positively affirm that life began in space (Heaven) where Jehovah presides and was successfully translated here on earth by the same deity. But we must at this point give a sound definition as to what life is. Let us for the purpose of soundness use the most literal definition of "a state of existence." Ephesians 1:4 gives us this universal spiritual truth, that *"He chose us in Him before the foundation of the world..."* God spoke to Jeremiah, *"Before I formed you in the womb I knew you..."* (Jeremiah 1:5). Second Timothy 1:9 propagates the major factor that we were not an afterthought, but we were ordained to be given the grace gift of salvation through Christ before the beginning of time.

The bottom line is, what is seen in the natural is already existent in the supernatural prior to its earthly expression. Thus man, salvation, the cosmos and every created thing had to exist before coming to the world to be alive in God and His Kingdom. *All* that was made was first created in God and, within the fullness of time, was birthed out of Him. However, we must not take this scriptural fact and make it say something it does not say. It does not say we enjoyed a pre-creation existence that took in actual manifestation and functionality in outer space or on another planet. (I'm not agreeing with the "big bang" theory as science relays it at all.) Instead, it is saying that whatever God desired to do, make or create already existed in Him. This is why everything about Him breathes life. Verses 9 and 10 of Genesis, chapter 1, express that God then separated the waters under the firmament from the dry land, calling these waters seas. This was accomplished within the framework of the time period identified as the third day. Is it too preposterous to believe that the landmass from which man was created was underneath those same waters prior to the sixth day?

The land was fertile with life, the very life of God spoken of in the "light" of day one. If science would permit itself to come into the knowledge of God, it would find that it can and will only confirm the truths already given by revelation to men contained within the Scriptures, just as Isaiah 40:22 long ago settled the issue of a square or round earth. These are but a few instances whereby scientific factual and not just theoretical findings harmoniously attest to the truth of the timeless revelation of God's Word. The closer the world gets to the truth, the more their search will end in the true and living God.

It is safe to believe that Christians are not insane or unsound for their belief in the accuracy of God's Word. We can follow through in speculation to summation that fallen man might assuredly have taken on a more bestial form while still retaining a thinking mind. It is scientifically known that man no longer uses the entire brain, as he obviously must have had the ability to do at creation. Consequently, the Genesis account of creation, the fall and foundation of civilizations of man (in my estimation), had to have taken place over millennia. When it becomes important for God to reveal all of this truth, He will do so, leaving no room for speculation or theories like mine. For now, the Scriptures we do have are more than enough to find factual answers to all things.

Chapter 5

The Covenant of the Fathers

Both men and women long for fathers, even though many humans' primary parental relationship is with a mother who is prominently involved in their lives. We often designate the dwelling place of our parents in modern western civilization as our mother's house more than the house of our father unless the mother is deceased. In ancient days it was quite the opposite, and the term the "house of my father" held a wealth of meaning. Because of Adam's abdication from his Heavenly Father, Satan, God's total antithesis, sought to pervert the institution that would be born and cause the Church to abandon its Father and the world to divest itself of the healthy establishment of fatherhood.

The word "father" has many reasonable definitions, among them being the literal meaning, a male parent, or the figurative meaning, an entity that is a cause or source. It is a title most often accorded great respect. Its panorama of terminologies takes in a plethora of nomenclatures from our forefathers to Catholic priests, and civic leaders to God Himself. Even women who are called to the apostolic pastorate are looked upon as "fathering" mothers in the most ingenuous way. Nonetheless, just holding the distinction of having the title does not make one a true father. This right of passage must be earned and acted upon to receive the admirable distinction this entitlement deserves.

The male human Adam contains, within the definition of his Hebrew name, the meaning "God's blood." This gives sound significance to the Father's need to have bloodshed become the prerequisite for the expiation for sin. Dr. P. A. Price, founder and director of Everlasting Life Bible Institute, Tulsa, Oklahoma, in expounding upon the scriptural revelation of life in the blood, teaches that in Christ there is spirit and life. The life-giving force that comprises the blood of mankind is genetically found in the male sperm. It is therefore safe to conclude that the spirit of man is also contained within that life-giving force.

The Master of the universe sets in motion spiritual laws that, if obeyed, will bring forth peace with God and the peaceable fruit of righteousness. If man lay with a harlot, the potential exists to procreate with that harlot excluding a legal, binding spiritual, covenantal contract, which sanctifies the seed as consecrated. This is why God demands holiness and expresses that lying with a harlot does not permit children to be born to that legal covenant between a man and wife. As is expressed in subsequent chapters, unholy unions leave a convenient place of access for unclean spirits to come for the children sired of the illegal union, with the parents already being a part of the seduction. Generational spiritual forces then may set themselves in position for a four-generation domination that can only be broken through acquiescence to salvation and sanctification. (On a positive note, these children can reach sanctification of their own accord by accepting the gift of salvation acquired through the second Adam. Even better, their parents who have received the Savior find forgiveness and benson [the blessing of forgiveness], offering the children a direct route to salvation and freeing these children from the curse of lawlessness.)

Such was the case with the first man, Adam. In essence, he was metaphorically married to Jehovah, his originator. By lying spiritually with satanic seductions, he defaulted in his position of spiritual purity and righteousness, resulting in the birth of the first child (followed by other ensuing children) filled with the unyielding seed of violence, death and destruction. This child was given over by his mother and father and was designated as the child of the wicked one. "God's blood" now had a son born to unholy parents filled with bewitchment, beguilement and ultimate defile-ment, allowing the desecration to take hold in the bloodline. The Apostle Paul affixes the chief blame upon the male, Adam, for the fall in Eden due to his extemporaneous acceptance of Satan's discourse. Adam, *being present with Eve* and the charmer, fell prey to the same seduction, but with the seed and spirits of all future generations of humanity in his loins.

 Herein is defined the phenomenal and wondrous mercy and love of our Savior. He still retains His covenant with man and woman and fulfills His Word to the nations. The Master continuously supplies food and drink from the earth and continues the race through fecundation (insemination). It is for this covenant right Jesus became the second or last Adam, rectifying the first's iniquity. He compassionately disregarded the thought of cursing the seed of the male lest He break His own treaty with humanity ratified in Heaven before the foundation of the world. Instead, the Lord implemented the law of blood covenant sacrifice for right retribution for sin, receiving it as a surrogate for His Son, which was to come. He straightway condemned the serpent and called the ground accursed.
The curse that falls to this day upon humanity is intrinsically tied to breaking the law, for the curse of mankind was in and of the law. Laws are created to give the righteous good conscience by showing right from wrong. When followed, there is no need for their penalty to be observed. When disobeyed, the virtuous followers place a demand upon them to punish evildoers. This is the true meaning of the curse. Who is more righteous than Elohim? Accordingly it is most sensible to follow the command of God than to disobey and reap the penalty. The gravest penalty of the law is the enforcement of death, which in its truest delineation means separation from God.

 Christ has redeemed us from the curse of the law *if* we accept His sacrifice and live by His command. He has so remarkably created a way by which we may experience the fullness of His love and longsuffering. As ministers of Christ's covenant, we must show the world the bountiful greatness of God's love toward them that they might be drawn by love and not fear. But this coin has two sides: We must also restore the fear of the Lord to His house, and the sanity and sanctity that come with keeping His commandments in love. The male of the species, human beings, enjoys a covenant with God no female will ever be able to enjoy. It was an absolute necessity to create the male first and take the female out of him for the reasons previously discussed. All spirits were contrived to follow the order of Jehovah, the divine Creator's principles. The spirits of all human offspring are contained within the male and subsequently make him the father of the mortal, bipedal species called man. The female therefore could not be created first as she is another complete "male" unit, only equipped to incubate seed.

It has been scientifically proven that the DNA for sanguine human fluid is contained within the male spermatozoa. Generally, lawsuits to prove parental rights are projected toward proving fatherhood and not motherhood. Referred to as paternity suits, these cases have been the origin of much joy, pain or disillusionment. After the birth of the child in question, the male's blood DNA is compared to that of the child in question. The latest forensic scientific data and equipment can unerringly predict the father within a 98 to 99 percent ratio of surety. This comprises the most resolute reason for the covenant of circumcision. Sin necessitated the shedding of blood over the reproductive organ of the male. It is a special covenant between God and men that sanctifies that area for the purpose of procreation. The "spirit" and body of the seed are contained therein making blood the most powerful substance in the universe. This fact is to be taken seriously by man, for God and Satan take it very seriously. Of course, it must be understood that circumcision is of the law, and we are no longer required to keep the letter in order 10 please the Father. However, the act of circumcision does carry health benefits and is still a requirement among many religious groups.

There is more than a perfunctory purpose for fathers carrying the genetics for blood; and that is God's decreed origins of humankind. If man did not have this exacting bond with his off;

spring, he would abandon them because of the fall, feeling little or no remorse. While there is much spoken of the intricate bond between mother and child, very little is ever cited in modernistic society regarding the bond between fathers and children. Of the many negative results of Eden's fall, perhaps the potential destruction of the bond between the male and his paternal offspring is listed among the most devastating. After the peccadillo in Eden, Adam found it comfortable to give Cain, his firstborn, over to Satan. Why? It is because of the disruption in the fatherly bond.

When Adam defected to another family, so to speak, he accepted the precepts of another father and proceeded to follow those new ordinances. The consequences of this action were inordinate. Firstly, God, Adam's father, was abandoned by Satan in Heaven, and consequently through seduction, caused Adam to do the same. Secondarily, Adam became angered at the first creature to be produced from his flesh and laid the total blame on her instead of the spirit behind the serpent. Lastly, Adam releases his seed into the womb of his wife producing a firstborn son who showed visible signs of rejection by his earthly father. Sibling rivalry is born as a result and murder becomes the irreverent outcome.

This degenerative state of the first father released a diabolical, implacable failure in the strain of Homo sapiens to parent, or in this case, father their offspring. It is only because of the tender mercies of the Almighty that this sin did not take root to the degree that detachment became the chief, irresolvable issue. Following God's laws provided a way of resistance and/or atonement to sin prior to Christ, and His supreme sacrifice enabled man to divorce this and all sin. Sad to say, whenever there is no proper sacrifice or acceptance of Jesus and godly values in a home, this woeful transgression resurfaces, being fueled by its father, Lucifer. Some would argue the veracity of this statement, but its truth is witnessed by the enormous feelings of desolation and abandonment present today in this generation. It may not always display itself in fathers physically abandoning children, but may be evidenced in poor parenting skills, child abuse, pedophilia, homosexuality and bisexuality, intimidation from one generation to another, lack of inheritance, unexplained anger and rage, divorce, etc. Its roots are seldom identified as a portion of the Garden's fruit relegated to fatherhood.

There are multiplicities of reasons for abandonment. We will examine seven of the most compelling.

1. The most prominent cause is due to the fall. Man too often attempts to do by the flesh what can only be done by the spirit. Humans were told to take dominion over the earth and subdue it, yet the curse of the ground gave rise to man neglecting his family in an attempt to subdue the earth. A single bite of the fruit of disillusionment devised chaos, allowing the fruit (of the ground) to subdue the dominators. Drug abuse, alcoholism, sickness and a ménage of other maladies all prove this indictment: Insubordination begets domination by that which should be under your feet. Man cannot take dominion by flesh, but must do so by piety, submission, hard work and balance.

2. Lasciviousness. Whoredom produces defiant offspring who bring a further anathema upon the land, inspiring the same loathsome behavior, which requires a purging of the earth by the Father. Beyond this, the seed is at risk for infiltration by the adversary. Immorality is the highest order of sin because it produces the possibility of offspring who are targeted by Satan.

3. Contempt for women, especially mothers. The Apostle Paul clearly dignifies the necessity for mothers and wives by stating by the Spirit in First Corinthians 11:12, *"For as woman came from man, even so man also comes through woman; but all things are from God."* This also can perpetuate throughout generations, for children mimic their first tutors. It can lead to other biblically nefarious practices such as bisexuality and homosexuality.

4. The absence of fathers in the preceding generation. The distress caused by this has been consequently explained and may lead to an emblazoned intimidation between one generation and its fathers.

5. The spirit of Cain was never addressed. Murder, sedition, sibling rivalry, anarchy and other forms of contumacy (resistance to authority) are under the criterion of satanic ascendancy. It is a critical issue that is a preeminent, numinous (ethereal) force over every nation. This encourages the exigency for punitive legal enforcements and harsh restraints. These dynamisms are rampant in every society.

6. Satan desires pluralism. Pluralism is the theory of beliefs incorporated in the essential to various systems of philosophy, that reality has its essence or ultimate being in several of many ethics or substances. Antichrist's categorical goal in this is to keep man in a frame of mind to have multiple variances of thought and actions with no absolutes. This destroys God's rule and at length the institution called fatherhood.

7. Sexual ambiguity. Homosexual marriages and homes are recognized unions, complete with adopted children in some cases.
-sexuality along with bisexuality renders civil the right to hold marriage according to Christian doctrine, as contemptible, unnecessary or inconsequential to life. Ambiguity in and of itself dissolves purposeful lines of demarcation, devastates normal sexual orientations and deifies abnormality. For Christianity, this is an abomination and deviation from the true purpose of man.

    As you can see in these seven particulars, Adam's sin demanded a colossal response from Heaven. It necessitated the blood covenants of circumcision and sacrifice and the unequivocal need for a savior. Another seldom discussed outcome of renunciation of the seed is refusal to father. A male who dies childless and non-canonized (in the truest sense of the word) leaves no testimony of his fatherhood in the earth, and divorces himself from the possibility of siring salvation through the preaching of his children, spiritual as well as natural. Such was the case with a biblical man named Onan whose name means vigor. Genesis 38 informs us that he was a son of Judah (Jehovah will be praised). Upon the death of his older brother Er, Onan was instructed by the Lord through his father to raise up children to his brother's childless widow, Tamar.

When it came time to marry and copulate, this son determined he would not obey a direct command, for he knew the heir would not be his but Er's. Instead, he ejaculated on the ground. Directly the Lord slew him. Deeply grieved, Tamar all but lost hope that she would receive children in this earth from the "Lion of Praise." Judah instructed her to await the growth into manhood of his third son Shelah, and she would be given to him. However, disobedience seemed to have passed legitimately from father to sons, for Judah also would not keep his word after Shelah became a man.

Years passed and Judah's wife died also, and he left and went to the threshing floor to grieve. When it was told Tamar, she cunningly dressed herself as a harlot and met her father-in-law on the way. He came into her tent to lie with her, but before intercourse, she extracted a pledge and tokens from him; he would send her a kid from his flock (a sacrifice), and she in rejoinder, would return his signet and cord (the official seal of his authority as an honorable man of position along with the cord from which it hung about the neck) and staff.

She became pregnant with twins and appeared unabashedly in public. When it was told Judah, he sent for her to have her burned for playing the harlot. Isn't it a sad imputation against Judah that he would not submit himself for punishment or in the least, display remorse before God for committing the sin of which he accused her, yet demanded her loathsome execution? Instead, his ego and reputation as the living father had been reproached and he desired her life in retribution. She was willing to acquiesce to his demand, but first took the liberty of presenting the tokens to him given her by the father of her children. Judah acknowledged them, declaring her more righteous than he, canceled her execution but never went into her conjugally again.

It would only be an intriguing, brutally loveless story of lust and misogyny were it not for the tremendous lesson to be learned. Tamar gave birth to twins, Zerah (dawning, one who comes first). and Perez (a breach). These were not just any twins, for Mathew 33 lists them in the genealogy of Jesus Christ, the son of David! Judah behaved irresponsibly and acted as a poor father and leader by not keeping his vow before the Lord. Despite Judah's inadequacies, the Lord obtained what he desired; the dawning that covered (came before) the breach, prophesying in a nuance that Jesus was the dawning of salvation and the only bridge to once and for all bridge the breach between God and man.

Vietnam

A critical force that has assaulted societal norms that define fatherhood and family as are upheld in the Bible is the inauguration of war. The last notable war of the 20 Century was Vietnam, a civil war costing in excess of 58,000 American lives. Whenever mankind enters into an unjust action such as was this war, the spirits of darkness take advantage of the chaos spawned. The negative results were a generation of Americans who rebelled against the status quo because the fathers of the nation could not be trusted. This war was an important war, for spiritual forces were dictating to my generation to defy the living God, experience free love (lasciviousness), divorce the traditional church, take drugs, drink alcohol, smoke cigarettes and much marijuana, die young and make a pretty corpse. Culture wreaked the defiant attitude and has attempted to repeat the decade of the 70's that has given rise to it ever since.

Some 58,000 "generations," so to speak, were wiped out in less than two decades of war. Those men and women fortunate enough to return were treated to an abhorrent degree with contempt by society and the system. The spiritual forces behind abandonment reigned supreme and many "baby boomer" children born in that period reflected the attitude of trauma inflicted upon the generation. Male parents felt detached from their children, and the children as adults perpetuated the action. Simultaneously, God countered by reawakening a mighty revival in America among "Hippies" and American youth in the "Pop Culture." Young people were being baptized in the ocean, swimming pools and churches by the thousands, not shrinking away from demeaning descriptions such as Jesus freaks, zealots and religious nuts. *The* Father had to save the institution of true fatherhood in the midst of chaos. Though Vietnam was unsuccessful in its initial aim, God's revival and consummate sweeping move of massive salvation of the lost became a historical evolution in the ability for the survival and perpetuation of the good news, proving Him to be the Father of life and lights.

We must acknowledge and understand that God's laws and His Spirit make it possible for even an unsaved father to bear children who will become Christian and thus become the salvation of generations to come, all through the legal marriage covenant. This is a sobering argument for Christ-centered marriage and, if unmarried and childless, fathering the generation at hand. It is even possible for a man of marital covenant, even *unsaved*, to transcend the ungodly principle of offspring abandonment, finding peace with the God of His spouse, particularly if he is married to a wife who is a true believer. The scripture distinctly recounts that a wife may win her husband by her "chaste conversation" (godly lifestyle and communication) according to First Peter 3:2, and the unsaved spouse is consecrated by the saved. *"Otherwise your children would be unclean..."* (1 Corinthians 7:14). The same principle applies to the unsaved wife.

The Father never intended for fathers and their children to be separated. Instead, by design, He shrewdly and calculatedly devised a bonding that could only come by blood, and since Adam's very name contains blood within its definition, the Lord caused His covenant to prevail beyond the sin of man to produce His desired result. This is the greatest and clearest argument for the fact that God did not and would not curse the male or the female, but instead made provision in advance for sin to be punished and conquered. The curse is of the law and it is enforced upon those who refuse to uphold it; the lawless are damned. God still enforces the right to claim the seed of any generation and thus will exercise His right to bless to a thousand generations. Conveniently, His wisdom has clearly made it virtually impossible to have any entire generation that is void of the possibility of salvation, for in the Almighty's cycle of life eternal, there can never be a thousand generations of the condemned.

Chapter 6

God's View of Fatherhood

"Even though you have ten thousand guardians in Christ, you do not have many fathers…" 1 Corinthians 4:15 NIV

If you are as blessed as I am to have a good father, you recognize that just as the Proverbs 31 woman is a combination of all the qualities listed, so is a virtuous father. He is sincerely worth his weight in gold; his price is above rubies. My roots are nothing short of miraculous. My father, Attorney William Green of Youngstown, Ohio, was born to unknown parents and abandoned in a railway station in Waycross, Georgia, in 1923. The couple who found him saw that he was a beautiful baby and they requested to adopt him.

In the 20's in America, a black child was not considered of as high value as a white child except in the black community. Also, in those days the church was the hub of that same society. A person would be considered an infidel if he abandoned his family, and a heathen if he never attended church, unlike today. Black children were seldom homeless, crowding out orphanages, and the community did its best to make provision for each child to have a home. Ordinarily the placement for a child whose family was unknown would be commandeered through the local church, but in this case, it was not done according to social custom. If you were unfortunate enough to suffer the loss of your family as a child, other relatives, neighbors or even strangers would adopt you or simply take you in, in the black community. Therefore my father's adoption by strangers was not unusual. My adopted grandfather never relayed any information to my father as to the identity of his parents. Of course, in those days people kept secrets to the grave, particularly if the secret concerned family or was dark. Everyone who may have been able to shed light on the subject is now dead, leaving the natural mystery unsolved, but the spiritual mystery alive and ongoing in Christ.

William Green, Sr. had a wife with a heart full of love to give to children, but little health to bear her own. It only took a few weeks for the process to be completed and the would-be orphan found himself in the company of his adoptive parents and another older girl (also orphaned) heading toward Pennsylvania and eventually Youngstown. It is in Youngstown that the wonder of the Heavenly Father unfolded to keep a male child alive to see his generations. His first mother died when he was about two. (Sadly, his sister died also before she was nineteen years of age.) His father remarried a shrew of a woman who put him and my father through abject domestic horror. By the time my father was twelve, she had perished and the future attorney was forced to take care of a home as best he could and find direction in life any way possible. At age four the Lord gave my father an apparition imparting to him the sequential evolution of his life's journey. He saw that he would become a lawyer, would marry and have three children by his wife. As remarkable as this sounds, the little man believed it to the extent that he would sneak into the courthouse and watch cases when he was less than ten years old.

The prophecies happened with alarming accuracy, for he married a remarkable woman, Dorothy Wigfall, and sired three beautiful children by her (one now deceased along with my mother), each apostles and prophets, and grandchildren besides with prophetic, ministerial, musical and business callings to name a few. This is the astonishing power of divine predestination. The Father knew that He needed to give birth to a dynasty of prophetic voices and in the fullness of time, arranged for a couple with capacious hearts to adopt children of unknown origins, taking them to their Jerusalem. My brother, nieces, nephews and I are functioning today because of the Lord's kindness to grant my father clandestine favor. No entity of ours would exist had my father not survived. He raised us with a fortitude that said, *do not abandon your seed and never give up on your dream.*

My father is a real father, though not a perfect one, and is an example of miraculous intervention coupled with incomprehensible divine orchestration. William Green follows the mandate of God to this day, realizing the power of His Spirit to set in motion divine destiny and has totally submitted to Christ's authority for more than twenty-four years. This says to us that God's orchestration of our lives is heavily based around our roots and origins, but not from a natural perspective over a spiritual one. God was at work on our behalf and on behalf of His Kingdom before we were even remotely aware of it, making this story a noteworthy example of the virtues of fatherhood and heavenly grace.

The Fatherhood of Abraham

It must be realized that God looks at fathers much differently than others. Abram cut a covenant with God in Genesis 15 that brought the birth of the promised seed, Isaac. Abram seemingly had little difficulty hearing the voice of the Lord by this time, for God tried him exhaustively before trusting him with this extraordinary covenant. There was no sparing of Abram; his trials were difficult, rigorous, and to all appearances, unrelenting. However, with each trial was an equal measure of blessing. Each was gravely calculated to subdue all fleshly ambition, demanding the prophet to yield every dream to absolute contrition. Only when Abram was too physically weak to rise of his own accord did God put him into a death sleep, cutting an unbreakable covenant with Himself over the prophet's body. This man of the wilderness passed every test, yet in all this his humanity permitted him to create an Ishmael.

It is important to recognize the fact that Jehovah, a good shepherd, personally knows His sheep. Abram first recognized in Scripture as God's prophet (by the name prophet), was underdeveloped to a great extent, and while we may deem his trials too severe, they were in particular what he needed to rise above circumstances and be developed into the "father of faith" his destiny demanded. The Father is aware of what may make or break us as individuals. These trials only did Abram good, for it birthed in him the kind of spirit that would be obedient to God in all things, even if it meant the sacrifice of his son.

Abram was chosen because God knew he would raise his children in the admonition of the Lord. Like any good father, it was difficult for him to release his error, Ishmael, into the hands of the Lord to allow the promised child to grow before him in peace and safety. He was told to hearken to the voice of his wife in the dispelling of the bondservant and her child. The first man to hearken to the voice of his wife caused death and condemnation to fall upon mankind. This woman's advice was according to covenant laws and was every bit as much a prophetic act as their receiving the vow of Isaac's birth. God is making an impressive statement:

Woman was not solely responsible for the fall of man, neither is she incapable of blessing men with her leadership abilities and wisdom. It is an extraordinary act of faith to give our failures over to Messiah, particularly when they are robed in our flesh. He is the only One who can cleanse and redeem, restoring them to us healed and blessed. Jehovah made of Ishmael a great nation because he contained within him a measure of his father, a righteous man, and the seed of his generation that may find the way of salvation. God's immeasurable love was displayed through the multiplicity of times Ishmael's children were responsible for saving the lives of Isaac's seed, resulting in the covenant of both sons being fulfilled. Among the most dramatic was the sale of Joseph to the Ishmaelite traders bound for Egypt.

Genesis 37:25-27 KJV states:

"And they sat down to eat bread: and they lifted up their eyes and looked, and, behold, a company of Ishmaelites came from Gilead with their camels bearing spicery and balm and myrrh, going to

carry it down to Egypt. And Judah said unto his brethren, What profit is it if we slay our brother, and conceal his blood? Come, and let us sell him to the Ishmaelites, and let not our hand be upon him; for he is our brother and our flesh. And his brethren were content."

A notable Archbishop of the Syrian Orthodox faith, His Eminence Veron Ashe of Fresno, California, said, "It was a necessity for our sovereign Father to purge Ishmael from the loins of his father that the son of the promise might be brought forth in due season both in purity and in purpose!"

The Fatherhood of Noah

Noah was a man of ridiculed faith. He preached a searing message of judgment for 120 years, winning no converts. God destroyed the earth and vowed never to repeat this form of abrogation, leaving only Noah and his children alive. We as the church make the doleful error of thinking that because Noah's sons were saved through the Ark that they were obviously in agreement with God. However, there is little to nothing that even implies the sons were virtuous, but the father was.

To prove the inference, Noah's son Ham committed an outrageously blasphemous act against him; he mocked his father's nakedness. This takes on a new connotation when we consider the fact that Noah had risen from merely being a father to becoming *the* covenant father of the existing world, and the world to come millenniums beyond. It escalated his significance in the heavens as also his authority on earth. The spirit world awaited his decrees. In violating his father, Ham brought desolation to humanity overall. He also severely affronted the sanctity of his own mother and father's covenant, for she was also biblically symbolized as her husband's nakedness. One futile act of disdain brought repugnant grief to many generations to come.

Engrossed in the sorrows of having to say farewell to all he had ever known except his family, Noah went beyond the correct measure of wine and polluted his soul into a false sleep. Noah lay naked and vulnerable to the spiritual forces of the universe and his son could only look upon him with disdain. He needed to cover his father. But when this fallen, grievous father was the most defenseless, his son did not defend him. To Ham, Noah was the reason for the destruction of all he had known in life, save for his wife and children. Not only had he suffered the term of one full year on the Ark under Noah's rule, but also all hope was dashed when he could finally return to land to find all humanity was gone. His sin led to the chastening of the Lord through a lesser lord, but great ruler in the earth, his own father. Had not all other older men died, Noah would not hold the exact same authority in Heaven and earth, but all others died at the command of the Almighty, making Noah the oldest living father of mankind. He was now in the place of Adam. The weight of that fact was overwhelming.

Noah said, "Cursed be Canaan," not "Cursed be Ham.' Canaan was the land and the inheritance given to the children of Ham, or Ham's present inheritance. This is a Kingdom judgment and could only be evoked in a Kingdom manner. When the land was given into the hands of Israel, the curse was fulfilled. Ham had sons who did rightly in the sight of God and were inducted into the house of Israel to inherit a portion of the land that was initially theirs, for God only visited their sin to the prescribed generations. Therefore, there is no such thing as the racist, heretical doctrine of a Hammedic curse. All lawlessness is punished by the curse of the law and not by race. Ham was darker black, but no better or worse than the other sons who would be considered biracial by today's standards.

Long after the death of Noah, a race of giants evolved in the earth who were mutated, repulsive deviations from human form and survived the floods in the loins of Noah's sons. Goliath of Gath was such a man. This aberration from the original intent of the flood proved that one small amount of taint in the seed prior to Christ's redemptive blood could cause monumental problems in the bloodline. This is a grave argument for the purity of fatherhood. God knew the next desolation had to destroy systems and not bodies alone, rendering the soul to rehabilitation and reconstruction. God set the apostolic law of creation in motion: Men (and women) of the omnipotent Father would build the people; the people would build the Kingdom.

Malachi Predicts the Restoration of Fathers and Children

Jehovah knew the absolute necessity of His relationship to humanity and man's relationship to Him being carried out according to His Word. After the fall in Eden, God's master plan was still enacted on earth, for He had made provision for it before the worlds were framed. Foreknowledge permitted the Prophet Malachi to release the word of the Lord concerning restoration between natural fathers and children and our Heavenly Father and His children. Restoration does not mean to bring it back to its former state, but rather to make it better. Examine the words of Malachi in chapter 4, verses 5 and 6:

Behold, I will send you Elijah the prophet before the coming of the great and dreadful day of the Lord. And he will turn the hearts of the fathers to the children, and the hearts of the children to their fathers, lest I come and strike the earth with a curse.

The precognitive warning takes in far more than meets the eye. It speaks of the coming of the Prophet John whom Jesus identified as Elijah who was to come, and the impending disastrous judgments that would occur prior to and after the coming of the Lord as Savior. If John had not preceded Jesus, the generations would not have realized that Malachi's predictions were being satisfied through Christ. However, it foretells the coming of *"the great and dreadful day of the Lord"* after this event, a day which we are experiencing now. This is an announcement of tribulation following the restitution of fathers and children.

Jesus has already appeared once and will appear again shortly to reconvene His Kingdom forever. His death, burial and resurrection was the restoration prophesied. In the preparatory move He is emphatically putting into practice the refurbishment of divine relationship between the Church and the Father. We will see a revival of knowledge of the true and living God as Father sweep through the nations, destroying falsehoods for faithful believers. As the world becomes increasingly darker, we who are of the light will shine brighter as children of that light. Jehovah is the Father of the universe, but this time it will be acknowledged according to understanding. God will always respond to His fatherly duties and will never abandon His purposes or pursuits. This is His promise to His children. Fathers of the covenant possess the Kingdom right to make this happen by standing in right relationship with Jehovah and giving parturition (birth) to these plans and purposes of God. Only the righteous in ancient Israel could sit at the gates of the city and judge the unrighteous, executing punishment, even unto death. But when Israel played the harlot, the seed were the first to suffer, for the corrupt fathers who sat at the gates of the city brought the judgments of man instead of emitting the laws of God.

Jesus destroyed the foundation of the Pharisaical laws and resurrected the laws of Moses so that all men might see the error of their ways and submit themselves to be the fathers and leaders they were created to be. Now through Him we no longer labor under the penalty but conceal the laws of Jehovah in our hearts so as not to desecrate the inviolability of Christ's sacrifice.

Chapter 7

The Covenant of the Woman

"And I will put enmity between you and the woman, and between your seed and her Seed; He shall bruise your head, and you shall bruise His heel." Genesis 3:15

The first real promise or covenant toward mankind from the Father was in Eden after the fall. God spoke to Eve promising her Seed's victory over the followers of the serpent. This declaration was made in the heat of the most desolate historical moment for mankind. There was no condition given to Eve and Adam for this covenant's fulfillment. Jehovah took the entire onus upon Himself exclusively making it unconditionally true. He has capably brought this promise to fruition, for it applies to both world systems headed by demonic powers and individuals who work in darkness. Eve's children will give the final deathblow to their enemy, Satan, concluding the millennial reign of Christ. Death, hell and the grave will be consumed for the last time in the depths of the pit of hell, and the "Seed" of the woman, Christ, will rule and reign forever in the earth.

Woman, or man created with womanly characteristics such as a womb and paps, is the personification of the procreative part of Jehovah. She is not an entity that was designed to stand alone; neither was her corresponding partner. The female was created as the glory of the male just as the male is the glory of God. Both were told in their beginnings that they were created in the likeness and image of God. God created them and called their name Adam. Woman had to have a separate spirit and body to bring completion to the purpose for the man. This is specifically why the Apostle Paul in First Corinthians 11 refers to her as *"the glory of man."* Together they comprise "human," *H'Adam* in Hebrew, which is rightly understood by the full definition of Adam's name: God's blood, red, ruddy, earthy, man. *They* are the blood (light) made of the earth and can only be such if they are united as one. This statement incorporates far more than merely marriage alone, but encompasses that which causes peace in the spirit realm because there is peace between the corresponding representatives of Heaven on earth.

After the fall in Eden, God gave woman the first recorded promise of redemption. Hope labored alongside sin, disgruntlement, curses and shamefacedness. This hope was not deferred, making the heart sick, but it was an undying hope, unchanging. God promised Eve that her Seed would bruise the head of the serpent. The reference to the Seed is, of course, Christ Jesus, but encompasses far more than Christ in the flesh. This agreement identifies the children of the Seed, who are Christ's children. However, before the woman would be permitted to see this gratifying victory, there would be suffering: *"I will greatly multiply your sorrow and your conception…Your desire shall be for your husband, and he shall rule over you"* (Genesis 3:16). In my book, *For Women Only*, I cover the issue of women in every facet more thoroughly. It is a suggested reading to enlarge your understanding of the woman's covenant.

The phraseology announcing the rulership of the male was not a direct command given by God, but a description of the response given by the Creator to the sin committed. This cause now carries over into the promise relayed above, for if the Seed of the woman did not also die for this punishment, what did He die for? From the moment Eve concurred with the serpent's rhetoric, she became the most desirably undesirable and simultaneously revered creature in the universe. Every society in every nation in every generation has persecuted her, despite the seasons in which she is worshiped. But the benevolent Father who saw her (their) weakness and need in advance, made provision for her survival and ascendancy.

In Genesis 2:7-9, God placed Adam into a deep sleep and took a single fragment from his side. He then took the chemical composition of the flesh close to, but not part of, his heart and sculpted a creature who is mysterious, holy, perfect, and sexually pleasing. Because she is taken out of him instead of being made from a separate plot of earth, she is *"bone of my bones and flesh of my flesh..."* (Genesis 2:23). The aesthetic mischief of my fertile imagination always causes me to think that God knew Adam would attempt to presuppose how His handiwork should be hewn, and thereby bought himself a heavenly sedative that would preempt his meddling. Ah, but what joy he received upon awaking!

But that joy was short-lived, disrupted by the serpent's beguilement. In this fall, woman is singularly blamed by man, causing the announcement of his conclusion for the need to dominate her to frightfully come to fruition. The tug-of-war between God's male and female creation has given rise to a billion-dollar counseling industry, wars, murders, seditions, power struggles, deviant sexuality and countless books. It also has adversely affected that which is legally right and righteous in the ecosystem of God's planet, for animal life that man was told to dominate, unwittingly turned against man and other creatures according to the discord released in the spiritual and natural realms. Nature became disruptive and sometimes destructive in every facet of organic life. A diversity of matter spawned from the earth seemingly turned to challenge mankind, causing the earth to yield "thorns and thistles" and mankind to toil and labor by the "sweat of his brow" to garner food and provisions for his family.

Women are mediums of salvation through a most unpredictable source: the womb. This uncomely, hidden, vital organ was the central object of Satan's desire for woman. It is interesting to note that women can still live without a womb (the surgical removal is called a hysterectomy), and yet salvation could not exist without one. The Apostle Paul writes in First Timothy 2:15 of woman, *"Nevertheless she will be saved in childbearing..."*

The very womb that caused the fall became the very womb that fostered, nurtured and gave birth to salvation. In other words, a woman's procreative abilities make her invaluable and thus a precious necessity to the subsistence of life itself. Further, no matter how unlovely a woman may appear to be in one culture, there is a culture that will find her pleasantly comely. These, and so many other protective attributes, are given her to insure her success in surviving despite persecution. Jesus the Christ was born an issue of God and a woman, eliminating the provision of male intervention in this Immaculate Conception. His lineage after the flesh secured the inclusion of every race, kindred and tongue in every generation through His genealogy, suffering man to be restored to the Father through His passion.

The Sons of God and the Daughters of Men

In Genesis, chapter 6, a strange account is given of the "sons of God," who for all intents and purposes are not clearly defined. The first scripture designates the time period as being when men began to multiply upon the earth. This designation does not stipulate the manner in which the reproduction has been accomplished, and the concept of marriage being the chief vehicle is conspicuously omitted in the opening statement. The conjecture to the sons of God theologically spans two main schools of thought: One considers them humans who worshiped God and the other supposition proposes them to be angels. I take the latter stance for argument's sake. These angels in verse 2 observed the daughters of men and *took* them wives of all they chose. The word for "took" in this capacity means to seize, snatch or carry away as well as the accepted definition of to take a wife. The use of terminology here connotes a seizing as if by force more than the giving in marriage.

It must also be understood that these females did not necessitate a marriage covenant to enter into this relationship. It is not known whether they were willing or unwilling. If they were seized as I believe, they may or may not have assented to their seizer. Verse 4 informs us that there were giants in the earth in those days and *after* those days. What does this mean? Giant creatures roamed the earth before and after those days, and men were among the giants (Goliath was such a monster who existed after the flood). After these angels *came in* to the women, giants were born to them, men of renown. *Yaabo'uw*, the Greek for "came in," has a most startling definition: to enter into, to go in, and to come in.

Literally, God tells us that these spirit beings came into or possessed the women, and when they lay with men, whether husband or male doxy, the children sired were ghastly mutants. This feasible explanation supplies a credible appraisal of the situation and well illustrates God's response to the event: He sent a flood and delineated the length of days for man. Had it remained the same length as their forefathers, man would have had centuries more to continuously devise wickedness. Satan's desire to be saved when the Messiah redeemed man, or else so pervert man that he could capture a high seat as Heaven's ruler, continues to be proven fruitless.

The "Wombed" Man

Woman has a wonderful sensitivity and flexibility that causes her to be able to endure grave hardships. There is an expansive capacity in her to receive the love of a man and regenerate that love in the form of children, dream incubation, homebuilding, nurturing, administrating and so much more. Though there are many facets that set apart the female from the male, there are not as many differences as have been commonly assumed. The greatest presumed difference is the myth that women are touted as being more "emotional" than men. In actual-ity, that which is concluded to be more emotional is actually a godly virtue that can spare her life: Women can experience an emotion and display or articulate that emotion in a manner that produces healing. It is postulated that a woman tends to be more emotional and thus prone to hysteria due to the fact that she possesses a womb. Does this mean that a woman who has suffered the loss of the womb in surgery or is born without this marvelous organ would be less prone or perhaps never prone to hysteria?

From whence do such illogical postulations emanate? Prejudices brought on from the curse of Genesis 3:16: *"He shall rule over you."* According to Spiro Zhodiates' *Hebrew and Greek Key Study Bible*, the words for "womb" are the Hebrew terms *beten* [womb, the innermost part, the bottom of the heart], *rechem* and *rachem* [mercy, pity or womb], and lastly *me'ah* [to be soft, intestines, stomach, the uterus]. *Beten* comes from the unused Hebrew root which means to be hollow. The essential meaning is interior.

Zhodiates defines the only three New Testament Greek words for the womb as: gaster [belly, with child, or womb], *koilia* [abdomen, belly or womb], and *metra* [the matrix, something that gives order or form to something within, womb]. Notice that the Bible never uses the Latin or Greek words for the adopted English word *hysteria*. *The World Book Dictionary*, under the definition for *hysteria* (the Latin term for womb), gives the Greek root word for uterus as *hystera*. The dictionary then enlarges our understanding of the prejudice formed against women by explaining that the "new Greek" used *hystera* for womb due to the notion that women were more prone to hysteria because of the [function of] the uterus. The uterus is a muscle and has no ability to secrete hormones but rather responds to the hypothalamus gland in the brain.

Ovaries secrete hormones and are responsible for the hormonal effects upon the body. That clearly allows the feminine body to appropriately respond in turn to the emission of the hormones, a natural phenomenon that is not dictated by a womb or the lack of a womb, Needless to say, God's initial intention for the definition obviously took in the meanings divulged above and not the prejudicial expression assigned to it centuries later by the Greeks and later western civilization. The latest scientific data supports that stereotypical descriptions of male-female differences such as women are more motionally hysterical than men, men are better at math, women at language studies, men are insensitive, women alone are nurturing, are pure illusion and mythology. The latest findings show that men, in regard to brutal contact sports and violent crimes of passion (mass murder, premeditated and temporary insanity crimes of murder), brawls, mob lynching, war charges, etc., show a higher propensity toward hysteria than any woman ever dreamed, making emotional hysteria, instability and over-emotional indulgences a human experience of both genders in relatively equal proportions.

God thus proves that such prejudgments are anti-productive to purpose and destructive to harmonious relationships between the sexes. In essence, they are disparaging tools for those who would perpetuate disunity by remaining willingly ignorant. The truth, if sought out, speaks for itself. Lack of communication is one of the worst violations committed against women, particularly verbal. Though abuse of this ability is abhorrent, the positive value of it far outweighs the negative misuse. Women must have communication that relays feelings of security for her and the children, love and warmth. When we receive this we effectively reproduce it in our lifestyle. When it is frustrated, that is communicated. Whatever is sewn is reproduced.

Covering

The concept of God is universal. Jehovah is not just the God of the earth alone, but of the entire universe. Every culture has an acknowledged or secret belief in a God who divinely intervenes, dictates, mandates or justifies human behavior or existence. Gods are created to answer complex, frightening questions concerning mortal existence, or perhaps to empower one element of society over another. Religion is idolatry's spiritual medium of advancement and becomes an enabler of satanic vision. This is why we must place our beliefs upon those things outlined for us in the Word of God. In doing this, we allow God to define Himself and then make Himself known to us personally. The issue of covering in the Church of Jesus Christ stems from a misinterpretation of the Apostle Paul's writings in First Corinthians 11:1-13. Paul begins with the admonition for the Church at Corinth (not the church universally) to *"keep the traditions"* (v. 2), and ends this section by saying if there is a contention he and his followers have *"no such custom, nor do the churches of God"* (v. 16).

Because of the strong need for explanation and justification resident within every human, religiosity is fueled by the misuse of correct stipulations. The Apostle Paul's writings in this context should never be interpreted as a manner in which to harness females under the dominance of male superiority. Many mainline denominations have so subjected women to the cruelty of male biases that they have actually espoused the superiority of the male over the female! This is done despite the scripture that says there is no male or female in Christ, but we are one. Females in the Body of Christ would be shocked and dismayed to find that many of the most celebrated male leaders hold this unfavorable, ungodly, rigid and sanctimonious viewpoint. It is sad to note that far too many women would not receive that this is true if they heard the words spoken from the very ministers' mouths. Many more know and hold these views to be true based on instruction and not prayerful study mixed with revelation.

We have accepted unacceptable human behavior over godly good sense because of classical conditioning. Centuries of deliberate misinformation have laid a successful foundation for such inadequacies. This has been easy to do since the fact that the major portion of the Body of Christ does not study or research truth despite the fact that we are admonished by Jesus (for the same reason He admonished the Pharisees to search the Scriptures. We are also commanded by God to "study to show ourselves approved unto God." (See 2 Timothy 2:15.)

First Corinthians 11:1-13 is a very familiar passage of scripture and is generally used to support the bondage and not the liberty of a covering. Paul is referring to the tradition of the Jews to demand a woman to cover her head while praying (or prophesying) in public, an expression of deference and submission to the males of her household as well as reverence to the Almighty. Also, a curious choice of words is espoused in verse 10 of that passage:

*"For this reason the woman ought to have a symbol of authority on her head, **because of the angels**."* In my estimation this is a direct reference to the Genesis 6 fiasco delineating the illegal relationship between the female and fallen angels. The criterion appropriately addresses the Father's desire to see women properly shielded from unusual, demonic spiritual invaders such as prevailed in Genesis, chapters 3 and 6.

The Apostle Paul further states that God is the head of the male and the man is the head of the woman. (Once again, a more thorough revelation is to be found in my book, *For Women Only*.) The word for "head" that is used is *kephale*, which means in the truest sense "source of derivation" and not authority. Paul is simply saying the source from whence the man came is God, and the male was the source God used to create the female. However, Paul continues by saying that the male is not independent of the female, or the woman independent of the man in the Lord. She came out of him but no other woman or man originated excluding the womb because everything he is speaking of proceeded out of God.

Paul makes reference to a man's long hair as being dishonorable to him, but a woman's is a crown of glory. Yet, everyone would agree that many notable accounts of Jesus pictorially crown Him with a thatch of long hair. This is a reliable, potential description of Christ, just as the custom changed for men and women in Paul's society. That is why he ends by saying there is no such custom in the churches or with us. Far less penalty is enforced upon a man of God with long hair than a woman of God without a religious version of covering. Even so, the false theorem upon which the philosophy is founded is not mentioned or deduced anywhere else in scripture, insuring the fact that it is simply a custom and not a truism.

    The issue of covering further became an implied prescript to the latter-day church that commands all people in the Body of Christ to be "covered" (in the most literal frame) by some other member of the Body. While this is an essential, the concept has distorted the original use of head covering in First Corinthians and has sometimes been abjectly used to subject any and every authority to the same kind of bondage as women. In reality, the enforcement of the rule is generally limited to women, undesirables or smaller ministries. It is seldom used in deference to powerful male leadership. The fact of the matter is, everyone should have some. one in the Kingdom of God to which they must answer for the sake of integrity. In this, we cover each other. There are chains of command that dictate fail-safe checks and balances. This is indispensable. It must be realized however, that everyone answers to God and that leadership in His Kingdom is corrected from Heaven down through equal or greater authorities.

Chapter 8

Women as Ministers

As a minister of over twenty-four years, I hold the male leadership of my life in very high esteem, having no problem subjecting myself to it as a female leader. I also have had the unfathomable experience of having wonderful, powerful men of God submit to the authority God has invested in me. It is a privilege and an honor to be in the ministry. But with all due respect to some of my male counterparts, the issue of women as ministers has never been an issue with God. I have heard every incredulous interpretation possible to justify the disqualification of women as ministers. It is my belief that if the male of the species, particularly those born again, would simply take the time to inquire of God and their wives, sweethearts, mothers, sisters and daughters as to what a woman's life is like, they would be duly amazed!

Even though I have personally experienced great prejudice, I have never permitted prejudices of any kind to prevent me from going on with my life, especially in Christ, and there are many women just like me. The prejudices that women have become numb to are unbelievable to their male friends and relatives until it is compared to the male experience. Every man is painfully aware of the wretched feeling of prejudice and bias, whether it comes through a bully, a cruel boss, a parent or society at large.

Magnify it and you get what women have been contending with from time immemorial. I don't intend to sound as though these kinds of prejudgments formed as weapons against any of us should be used as an excuse to waste our lives or to become bitter. My intention here is to draw attention to the fact that they exist to an even greater degree than we may want to accept. Biases will not go away until they are healed by the sacrifice of Christ. In the meantime, we as women must determine to walk in love and study our covenant in order to stop bias from becoming a formidable foe.

To begin with, the Bible offers no restriction for a female functioning in any authoritative position in the Body of Christ. John addresses the elect lady who was in the least a pastor and possibly an apostle. Paul commends to the church, Priscilla and Aquila, a husband and wife team, with a preaching wife and mother (the female's name being mentioned first generally connoted that she was chiefly the minister and he the assistant). Junia is listed among the apostles, and we have not even touched the ministry of the Old Testament matriarchal leaders such as Deborah, Ruth, Queen Esther, Huldah and Hannah, for example.

It is not needful to break down the multiplicity of Greek and Hebrew words that apply to authoritative positions in the church. It should only be needful to ask godly people to open their hearts to the Father and allow Him to issue correction against discrimination, for we all at one time or another have been victimized by either using it or by having it directed against us. When more men begin to avidly herald the cause of women's rights as well as human decency, the end of intolerance will dawn swiftly. Bigotry of any kind is disallowed in the sight of God. It destroys the cords of unity so desperately needed to accomplish purpose, staunching the flow of love and unity in His Body. We cannot continue in purpose and accomplish its aims without unity.

We must pose this essential question concerning women in ministry to gain a comprehensible understanding: Why would the Father choose women to fill every capacity of leadership and then call them accursed or second-class? Possibly the problem innately is that it is not believed that the Father has called or commissioned women for service to Him in *any* leadership capacity. When we present the problem in its truest light, the negative view appears to be quite illogical and heretical. God is not double-minded. Neither should we be.

There is a common teaching that expresses the predisposed belief that women can be leaders but not heads. If men desire to bring truth to the statement, then every woman abandoned by her spouse whether by death or divorce, is summarily due another spouse or male adoptee in the least. Furthermore, no woman should direct anything in the church or in the world after her salvation, even if it is over other women and girls. Male children must be exempted from her sin so as not to displease the Lord. Since this cannot, will not (and in certain situations, must not) always happen, women must of necessity head their single parent households and all other placements at the dictates of God, regardless of the reason for the situation. The truth is, many wonderful men and women have been raised by a single mother as well as by a single father and have fared well, and women with the express approval and calling of the Father have headed many remarkable organizations like ministries, churches and businesses.

Why bring forth this issue? One of the requirements for eldership as well as the ministry of the deacon and the bishop is predicated upon fulfilling the customary standard of being a good steward over your own home. What is leadership then if it does not often take in headship? Who holds the rulebook of qualifications for headship versus leadership? God has given us the manual in His holy Word that well defines every essential for both commissions. They are often one and the same. Therefore, He does not make a difference, lest He blaspheme His own rule with the Deborahs or Miriams of this world. God never dishonors His own Word. If there is an issue raised that the great matriarchs of the Bible had a male over their heads, it must be recorded as to why. Their society was totally male-dominant but, in the least, demanded women and children to be cared for, and ours does not. Nonetheless, when God appointed women like Deborah, there was no question of her authority and no mention of her husband's headship. There was simply no necessity to make it an issue in their stories.

Esther

The book of Esther advocates an essential canon of divine, covenantal relationship. Her Persian name "Hadassah" means myrtle, while her given name "Esther" means star. She would become a propitiation for her people and would rise as a star bringing deliverance. The myrtle tree was a type and shadow of the Jewish church, and it was also a tree of peace and solitude, favor and promised blessing for the Jews. Esther literally became their promise of peace and favor in a troubled land. This beautiful, intelligent and spiritual woman epitomized the truly submitted woman of God.

Esther was placed in a most impossible situation. The king of a vast empire required all the young virgins to be presented in a beauty pageant so as to give him a new choice of a primary wife in his harem. A humiliating situation at best for a Jewess, this woman, born to be a deliverer, willingly subjected herself to the torturous separation from family, friends and community. The favor of the Lord was displayed and the noble female received the honor of being the chosen, and this is why.

Esther, a prayerful woman, knew from the Lord her sufferings must be for a greater reason than what presented itself. Her attitude in adversity saved her life and the lives of her people, for she determined to present herself in the very best light before the king. Esther, a commoner, did not know the protocol or custom of royalty. Each woman who pleased the king at sight was preferred to the best place in the women's chambers in order to be prepared to go in to the king, if bidden. This woman did not rely upon her humble upbringing to prepare to be obtainable, but rather inquired of the trusted chamberlain as to what would please Ahasuerus. Most people do not consider that the fame of Ahasuerus' callousness had spread abroad.

Esther knew for the sake of self-preservation and for preservation of her family it would be best if she find a way 10 please him so as not to incite his wrath. This included hiding her nationality until the proper time. She submitted herself to six months of purification followed by six months of oil of myrrh with milk baths for beautification of skin and softness. The king would have been accustomed to women who were cosmetically and aesthetically pleasing and would turn away from one who appeared to be mundane and earthy, smelling of the fields.

If the woman going through purification had skin blemishes, sandpaper was applied to the skin to rub them out, followed by oil of myrrh to deaden the pain; in other words, each candidate had to go through the process. Also, during this process each woman would be in seclusion from public view. All of this was done just to please the earthly monarch. At any point she could be dismissed, no questions asked, or put through the peril of being given to an underling. Therefore, Esther's fate was in the hands of a cruel society, but God knew she was prepared to meet the need of the moment. Her covenant was intact and because of it, her future was secure.

Each of us must learn a lesson from Queen Esther: When we are to be revealed to the King of kings, we must beseech the Spirit of God to beautify us internally and externally, for He alone knows how to please our Heavenly King. We must submit ourselves to the rigors of purification and perfuming so as to have the attractive fragrance of His essence. We cannot afford to fight going through the process, for to do so would preempt our ability to rise to our purpose in the Lord. How wonderful it is for us to be conformed to His image by bathing in His quintessence. This is the true objective of covenant.

Tragedy quickly ensued as her elder cousin (surrogate father), Mordecai, is pursued by evil Haman to be arrested and put to death for not bowing in homage to him. Further, all Jews in the province were to be executed by edict of the king through Haman's manipulations. Mordecai implores Esther to entreat the king for mercy, which meant that she would have to place herself in lieu of possible execution if he was not pleased with her presenting herself to him unbidden. It was out of this threat that God breathed through Mordecai the faith-filled, fateful words, "For who knows if you were sent to the kingdom for such a time as this?" (See Esther 4:14.) Esther heard the Spirit of the Lord in that plea and literally placed herself between life and death to intercede for her people.

The queen does not turn away from God in the trial but turns to Him in fasting and prayer for deliverance. In so doing, she obtains favor from her husband and is able to get a counter-decree published that will insure a victory for her people. Whereas on the day designated to put the Jews to death by the sword, the counter-decree said the Jews were to be able to arm themselves against a now defenseless enemy. A critical issue is presented in this story that is worthy of observation: Whenever a king publishes a decree and places his signet upon it, the decree is binding. It can never be revoked. God's declarations are the same way, but this earthly king's decree was countered in the same way God's would be. The king signed a counter-decree. Prior to Christ's death and resurrection, God's Word declared that sin would bring death. Jesus was the counter-petition that was given to mankind that canceled our death sentence through His blood.

Esther's obedience earned her the right to be the subject of a great holiday feast, Purim, still celebrated in Israel and the Jewish religion today. Likewise, our obedience to receive Jesus causes us to be seated in heavenly places with Him right now, and entitles us to an accommodation at the Lamb's great feast! Esther's story divulges the basic tenants of a submitted life: obedience and reliance upon Jehovah for the direction of every facet in life. She so thoroughly trusted God that she placed her life in the hands of a heathen king, and his chamberlain, knowing that God Almighty would give her counsel through him as to how to win the heart of the king. She did not put herself first, but she considered the plight of her people under wicked, harsh rulership. By so doing, she engaged the aid of the Spirit of God in propelling her into heavenly destiny.

As each candidate prepared herself to be presented before the king, they were given servants and free reign to request anything they felt necessary to beautify. Esther did not rely upon her own inclinations but sought the counsel of one who had a long relationship with the ruler. The chamberlain could inform her as to the colors, hairdo, apparel and other such entrapments that would please Ahasuerus. He also could instruct her in the art of presentation whether verbiage or motion. She was smart enough to take advantage of the equipment given her.

As we walk out our covenant with God, our "chamberlain" becomes the Spirit of God who guides and directs us as to how to present ourselves before the King of kings. Each covenant partner must subject himself to a time of purification before the anointing and coronation are accomplished. In the truest sense of the word she is covered by Mordecai, her husband the king and the people of Israel. She is the only female type and shadow of the Messiah in Church history in that she spends three days wrestling with the grave, and obtains favor and victory to triumph over death personally for herself and her kinsmen. This begot a conquering resurrection from a sentence of death.

When this aristocratic woman presented herself unbidden before the king, her life was on the line. She did not gamble with human affection, but she displayed faith in God's divine providence. So strong was her conviction that she concluded that if the plan did not work, she was willing to die for it. We never really experience life until we are not afraid to die for that which we believe. In this we surmount death and are free to truly experience life.

As women of God, life affords us an array of challenges. Jehovah does not permit them to become an overbearing burden if we pray and seek His face as Esther did. There is a godly, elemental tenet involving women that should remain a standard throughout the generations of mankind. Elder women who are sober, diligent and living holy should instruct the younger in the art of conducting themselves with sobriety in God's house. Older, first-time mothers have tasted more of the bitter and sweet of life and can offer a child a greater understanding of the follies of youth. Virtuosity in a woman does not mean being dominated without complaint, but rising as a queen despite cruelty, sin and hopelessness. It is achieved by comprehending your true covenant rights and by filling the mind and spirit with the fullness of God. It is not clear by the Scriptures whether Esther learned such virtues from her mother or not, but it is very clear that she learned true submission and humility among her own people. She will be extolled as an example for years to come and so will we if we follow her example.

Ruth

No one book of the Old Testament offers as precious a revelation of divinely inspired, relational blessing than the book of Ruth. The history of the season in which this story was comprised is exhilarating though not so dramatic. It is normally viewed as one of the Bible's most fascinating romance sagas, but this portrayal is far from accurate. It is a story that digs much deeper into the structure of the Father's covenantal order than most may ever recognize. Ruth's biblical setting was in the time of the judges in which there were famines, civil wars, turbulence, apostasy, intertribal jealousies and grave oppression. A famine drove Elimelech and his family into the land of the Moabites who were time and again enemies of Israel. These people had ascribed to an unbelievable history. These unusual, arcane inhabitants were descendants of Lot, Abram's nephew. His daughters seduced him by drunkenness after Sodom and Gomorrah were destroyed and sired children by their incestuous relations with him. Unfortunately, Moab was Lot's son and grandson by his oldest daughter (Genesis 19). The Moabites hired Balaam to curse Israel through divination (Numbers 22) and were barred from participating in the national corporate life of Israel for not giving succor to Moses and the children of Israel when they fled the despotism of Egypt's Pharaoh.

"An Ammonite or Moabite shall not enter the assembly of the Lord; even to the tenth generation none of his descendants shall enter the assembly of the Lord forever; because they did not meet you with bread and water on the road when you came out of Egypt, and because they hired against you Balaam the son of Beor from Pethor or Mesopotamia, to curse you" (Deuteronomy 23:3-4).

Because of these grievous sins, the Moabites were not permitted to enter into the congregation of Israel to the tenth generation. We would not have a history or blessed covenant had the story of Ruth involved this portion of history alone. After the famine pressed Elimelech, his wife Naomi and sons, Mahlon and Chilion into Moab, Elimelech died. His sons grew up and took wives of what were considered by Israel detestable Moabites, greatly hated and also among the feared foes of Israel. However, before Naomi could realize grandchildren of her offspring, both sons expired also, leaving three doleful widows in the land of judgment.

Ruth and Orpah, her sister-in-law, set out with Naomi to return to the land of her origins, for she had heard that God had visited Israel with bread. Along the way Naomi persuades Orpah to return to the house of her mother, but Ruth clave to her, reciting a cadence of her love for Naomi and God that was so inspirational it is used in countless weddings to this day. **But Ruth said: "Entreat me not to leave you, or to turn back from following after you; for wherever you go, I will go; and wherever you lodge, I will lodge; your people shall be my people, and your God, my God. "Where you die, I will die, and there will I be buried.**

The Lord do so to me, and more also, if anything but death parts you and me." Ruth 1:16-17

This is the crux of the story of Ruth's extraordinary virtuosity; she chose to leave her nativity and follow destiny to the lineage of Christ. Our obedience of the moment has far greater scope and depth than that moment affords us to know. It would have been perfectly logical for her to return to her family and the worship of the god, Chemosh, but she chose the more difficult though rewarding path. When we covenant with our Father, the passageway to obedience is not always simplistic or self-aggrandizing, but if we follow it over vanity and recklessness, our conclusion will be as hers.

The two women return to Bethlehem where Naomi hopes to recover a small portion of the inheritance of her late husband. After arriving, the picturesque Ruth wisely inquires as to the nearest kinsman so as to glean from a field that would be favorable to her. Israeli custom dictated that a portion of the field should be left for the poor or hungry sojourners to glean. She finds favor in the field of a man named Boaz and is given large amounts of grain he advises to be secretly pedantically left behind.

When Naomi sees what bounty Ruth has been able to possess, she advises her fastidious daughter-in-law to go to the threshing floor of Boaz to inquire as to whether he will honor her with marriage. He agrees to do so if a nearer kinsman will not secure that right. What is not commonly known is the nearer kinsman, in order to do the right of husband by Ruth, would have to give a portion of his inheritance to the son of Ruth, and thus would not greatly benefit by so doing. He gives the right to Boaz and a marriage transpires between the two. After Ruth's visit to the threshing floor the benevolent Boaz suffers her to leave in the covert of night undetected in the hope that her spotless testimony of good worth would not become tainted.

This is not as much a romantic move on the part of Ruth as it is a wise move. She realized that her mother-in-law's family was blessed and prosperous. She hoped for children and did not desire to live in the hedonistic community of her birth. She further understood that by marrying a well thought of man of the community, it would insure her acceptance as a Moabitess into the congregation of the Jews. The fact that she would consider Boaz, now eighty, was to her approbation, for she was commended for not looking to the younger, more handsome men for inanity's sake. Therefore, wisdom spread her covering over her, for Boaz heard of her kindness and virtuosity and was greatly moved. He prayed that the Lord would reward Ruth for her kindness and steadfast love toward Naomi, and God did through him. Ruth came to Bethlehem-Judah (house of bread) impoverished, and gleaned in a field. She left Moab (God's washing pot) to follow after the Most High God and met her Boaz (fleetness) in the company of Naomi (God's pleasant one). She had transitioned through the grace of the Lord from being married to and mourning Mahlon (sickly) to owning the field she gleaned in as a beggar. All of this was the result of Ruth (friendship) prospering through the Father's everlasting covenant.

Her story continues in that she gave birth to a son by the name of Obed (worshiper) who begat Jesse (I possess), who gave birth to David (beloved), the king of Israel. Because of David, Ruth is listed in the natural lineage of Christ. Devoutness gathers to itself great reward, for all women are blessed by the wonderful heritage of the matriarch Ruth, for she through faith was able to bring the Moabites into the covenant of the elect. God would not recognize the sins of her direct forefathers because her faithfulness to Him preempted the curse. The Almighty looked through time and saw the King of kings and rightly denied the enemy access to His throne. God pulled her through His utter timelessness (as though He ignored the timing of her life and backed the future into her present bringing about the cleansing of salvation retroactively) and covered her "seed" that would bruise the head of the serpent repeatedly. Thank God for timeless covenants.

Women, Literally and Figuratively

Despite the desperate attempts of the unholy triune principalities of darkness and the misogynists of this world, women have risen into prominent function in the Kingdom of God as well as in the kingdoms of men. One of the greatest honors bestowed upon us as females is to have a rewarding relationship with a husband who shows the correlation between God's relationship with His wife, the Church, and His bride to come, the New Jerusalem. This makes marriage the splendid covenant that it is, regardless of the challenges. It is also for us, the raison d'être (reason for being) that validates the need for our existence, for we know experientially how to be a bride, but we learn how to be a wife. This says that women can learn how to abide in covenant as well.

There is a preponderance of information concerning women who are wicked or sinful, but not nearly enough written concerning positive images of women in God's Kingdom overall. The mother of Samson, Hannah (Samuel's mom), the widow of Zarephath who fed Elijah, the Shunammite woman whose son was raised by Elisha, Mary (Jesus' mother), Mary Magdalene, Anna the prophetess, Deborah, Dorcas and Lydia (business women), John's elect lady, and many, many more were virtuous women of faith who have earned a place in both natural and spiritual history. They have left a profound legacy of which we can be proud. Some are showcased in this book and others just men-tioned. It would be of great import for each of us to study thoroughly the valiance of great women so as to understand how God has covenanted with them for His intention.

Though insufficiencies are evident in relation to the positive consideration of women, Jesus contributed bountifully to that aim, constantly showing His lack of sexual bias and His sagacity as it pertains to fair play. Nothing demonstrates this fact better than the story of the woman in John, chapter 8 who was caught in the act of adultery. She is taken from her bed of infidelity and literally thrown at Jesus' feet. Crouching down, the Master begins to write in the soil a nondescript message unknown to any of us. Some speculated He might have written the names of her lovers, or symbols of the law of Moses that applied to her situation. Whether any speculation is truthful does not matter, for the legitimacy of the situation spoke for itself: The woman was caught in adultery and could not be an adulterer alone.

No man was presented to Christ, but knowing our Lord, it should be obvious to us that He also supernaturally knew the identity of her accomplice. In superb style, God in the flesh speaks the abiding word of conviction that leads to liberation and forgiveness: *"He who is without sin among you, let him throw a stone at her first"* (John 8:7). When all her accusers backed away, the task at hand was accomplished. He made His point and vindicated the low estate of women at the same time.

Women were apostles, evangelists, teachers, governors, businesswomen, preachers, prophets, queens, military leaders, counselors, judges, mercenaries, conquerors, intercessors, virtuous wives, mothers, sisters and kinsmen. They were fearless, first at the cross and tomb, supportive of their men, brave, honest and true, arduous merits seldom afforded to them but often afforded to men. This book celebrates a few of their stories, but all are to be extolled and admired for their contributions to our understanding of how to live and prosper in Christ.

Chapter 9
The Covenants of Abraham and Noah

Certain covenants bear recognition as to the vital essentiality for a redeemer. Our Lord builds His precepts line upon line. It is therefore quite imperative to examine the process by which our awe-inspiring treaty with Christ occurred. The early covenants of Abraham and Noah provide us with critical information concerning the intent of man as opposed to God's intention during specified sequences of time on the earth. Though portions of these distinguished men's lives have been previously explored from the standpoint of their paternity in the chapter titled "God's View of Fatherhood," certain aspects of their callings identify for us the intricacies of why they were chosen by God and how these two covenants are deeply intertwined. They are used effectively to set in stone the covenant of Christ.

The Covenant of Abraham

In the book of Genesis, chapter 15, God cut an everlasting covenant with mankind that came to fruition as the covenant that permitted Jesus to enter the earth millenniums later. Abram's story begins with his unique introduction to a deity with whom he was not acquainted. God presents Himself to the patriarch by giving him an elusive command to go out into the wilderness and wait, leaving his family behind. It is precisely the way of the Almighty to seclude us for a season when He is verifying our call. It behooves us to be in strict obedience to the orders or we will suffer the consequences as Abram did.

Genesis 12:1-2 says:

Now the Lord had said to Abram: "Get out of your country, from your family and from your father's house, to a land that I will show you. I will make you a great nation…"

Abram took with him Lot, his nephew, his father, Terah, and "all the souls which he had gotten in Haran," an infringement upon the direct order to leave them behind! They departed until they came to Canaan. Here God released the indictment based on His original plan upon the "father of faith." Terah died in the wilderness and Lot's prosperity as a nephew of the chosen one caused his growth to be so massive that he had to separate from Abram to end the land disputes amongst the laborers. Abram was forced into purpose and obedience, a lesson to us all. It is after this that God further instructs him to sojourn into the land of Egypt, a place he was quite reluctant to go, and for good reason. The Egyptians were a sophisticated, idolatrous nation who had no dealings with the God Abram was just being introduced to. Historically, they were no friends of the Chaldeans.

Egypt was populated first by the descendants of Ham, specifically Hain, a son of Ham and grandson of Noah. They lived in a rich agricultural state with wealth and resources in abundance. Egypt sported monarchs called Pharaohs, conducted trade and commerce with surrounding nations, performed great medical feats, delved into the darkest ritualistic religious rites, was well equipped for war, remained very territorial, and was respected or feared by the surrounding nations. Noah spoke prophetically, *"Cursed be Canaan,"* a grandson of Ham. Canaan should not be designated in this curse as the individual but as the descendants and landowners. Though Egypt was not one of the lands of the Canaanites given to the seed of Abraham, God's judgment was executed upon Egypt for other reasons, for it still fell within the confines of another prophetic avowal. The land of Canaan was given to Israel for Abram's sake but was licensed over to Abram's seed by Noah's prophetic word and covenant with God. Therefore, Egypt had to be spoiled to get the chosen seed out of her into the promised land of Canaan.

Abram's search for the one true living God ignited episodes of skepticism as to what is the correct manner by which to conduct yourself with this true God. Jehovah took everything in stride and permitted grievous circumstances to dictate to Abram the genuine path of righteousness. This son of a Chaldean idol maker was not presented to the Lord by his lineage, but was hand chosen and inducted because of his faithfulness and integrity. The Father would never proceed to do anything without strictly following His own Word that obliged His speaking it through the mouth of His prophets beforehand. This covenant through Abraham was not one that needed to be kept a secret from the forces of darkness. To the contrary, it was rather needful to loudly proclaim it in order to subdue and defeat darkness. Thus, it was openly communicated and consummated. Although Abram was the first to be proclaimed a prophet in the scripture, Abel and Enoch were considered by some scholars (myself included) to be the first to actually prophesy a thing as prophets.

The covenant of the prophet is a profound one that requires strenuous testing, the greater trials coming to those whose commission is superior. Abram certainly qualified. It would not be wise to ponder or theologically argue as to the origination of the famine that arose in Genesis 12:10, but it is worth noticing its convenience in coming just in time for compliance to be rendered to God's command. Also worthy of note is the fact that the tempestuous examination took place just prior to the cutting of a most vital covenant. Abram's fear of the moment proved to be as great as his faith, for he believed Pharaoh would seek after his beautiful wife for his harem and it was so. All of this built into him a monumental trust in the true Creator. The Lord visited Pharaoh in a dream commanding him to release the beautiful "sister" of Abram, also his wife. So all-encompassing was the strategy of God that Pharaoh not only forced them to leave the country, but also gave them an abundance of gold, silver, cattle and much substance besides.

Abram, an already wealthy man, became exceedingly wealthy! At the end of our obedience is a profusion of supply and blessing. When Abram returned from his excursion into Egypt, he found that he had returned to the exact region he had initially left. However, both he and Sarai returned more knowledgeable about the wondrous Lord who was now guiding their lives on a course of which they had never dreamed.

God's covenant with Abraham actually began with these tests of faith and obedience. By the codification of the covenant Abram had successfully developed a strong faith that would carry him through the most difficult of trials: the requested sacrifice of his son, Isaac. On the morning of the formidable agreement, he girded himself in a loin cloth and began the sacrifice. By noon the vultures were fighting and scratching him mercilessly in an attempt to devour the dead carcasses. At the point that the Father appeared, Abram had fallen wearily into the center of the remains. To the Lord, Abram's bruised, blood-stained body lying as though mortified atop the sacrifice, reminded Him of His Son's sacrifice which was to come. The Bible states that a smoking furnace and a burning lamp passed between those pieces. God the Father, the Word and the Spirit agreed over the ostensibly dead body of Abram that His covenant would never end. The Father knew the frailty of man and would not take a chance of mankind infringing upon another covenant. When He could swear by no greater, the New Testament bespeaks the Lord swore by Himself that through Abraham He would bless, multiply and not curse. Our Lord knew that Abram could be trusted to raise his children to know the Lord, and as the faithful we today are being reared in the ways of the one true God through Abraham's testimony and covenant.

With the rendering of this covenant Abram (exalted father) and his wife Sarai (princess), underwent name changes to *Abraham* (father of multitudes) and *Sarah* (noblewoman) after the ratification. Each found it easier to obey in all things, and Abraham found the grace to take Isaac the son he had long awaited to the mountain of sacrifice. God provided a ram, and the father and son were restored to their family due to the faithfulness of God and the power of covenant.

The Covenant of Noah

Whenever a Christian views the beauty of a rainbow, this next covenant should come to mind. Noah was a man who lived in a turbulent season. The people of the world labored under the weight of mass confusion, idolatry, lasciviousness and greed. Their desire was to please the flesh continually. The New Testament warns of the ghastly consequences of disobedience to the moral structure of God's Kingdom. Romans 1:31 KJV warns that such a generation is without natural affection, and Romans 1:28 KJV says God gave them over to a reprobate mind. Almost certainly, the most telling and convincing are the references given by Paul to Timothy in 2 Timothy 3:1-5 and Colossians 3:5-7:

But know this, that in the last days perilous times will come: For men will be lovers of themselves, lovers of money, boasters, proud, blasphemers, disobedient to parents, unthankful, unholy, unloving, unforgiving, slanderers, without self-control, brutal, despisers of good, traitors, head-strong, haughty, lovers of pleasure rather than lovers of God, having a form of godliness but denying its power...
2 Timothy 3:1-5

Therefore put to death your members which are on the earth: fornication, uncleanness, passion, evil desire, and covetousness, which is idolatry. Because of these things the wrath of God is coming upon the sons of disobedience, in which you yourselves once walked when you lived in them.
Colossians 3:5-7

I chose the New Testament rather than the Old to display the truth about this pensive thought: *These things caused the destruction of the entire world in Noah's generation.* They also exist to an even larger degree in the New Testament era and unfortunately are quite prevalent today. The warnings are as pertinent now as ever, for we stand in lieu of witnessing the devastation spoken of in John's Revelation for the exact reasons as were set out by Christ, forcing us to gain an understanding of Noah's covenant. Jesus warns us in Matthew, chapter 24, that in the end times it will be the same as in the days of Noah. People will be marrying and giving in marriage, carrying on a normal routine, and will not observe the times and seasons. Suddenly Jesus will return as a thief in the night catching many people unprepared. We must be ready, for the tribulation of which He spoke is at hand!

To begin with, Noah was a righteous man though not a perfect one. He evidenced a sanctified lifestyle void of the assistance of an indwelling savior. The reason for his success could be totally ascribed to the enormous capacity shown by the Father for loving and providing supernatural abilities for all those who believe in Him on either side of the cross. Noah's faith transcended time and space, encompassing a superb trust that resulted in the salvation of the *guilty* and not just the innocent. The greatness of this covenant (and the tantamount reason for its mention) is the pertinent fact that Noah's consecration was the salvation of his sons and family and thus the entire human race after the flood. This concludes another fundamental reason for covenant: the enforcement of righteousness through the following of God's universal laws.

It is thusly the nature of our Savior to permit each Old Testament prophetic covenant to mirror His sacrifice that was to come. In the case of Noah, the ark of safety for his family is a representation of the most vivid prophetic symbolism: The substance wood used in one man's boat and life preservation was another man's instrument or death and torment. Both became a source of preservation for humankind. In the case of the cross and the ark, those who rode the waters of affliction were spared death, while He who received the waters of affliction made an ark of safety, reconciliation and restoration for those who believed and got on board.

Noah was a type and shadow of the promise that was to come in Christ. When a shadow is present it forebodes the fact that the object that casts it is near. A shadow is impossible without the presence of light. Since there is no time (as we know it) in Heaven, earth was bearing witness to Heaven's projection of the Almighty's presence, the Holy Spirit casting His great shadow. Through a multiplicity of types and shadows, God made a clear statement of His original intention. His plan was salvation, and systematically He brought the spiritual climate of the earth to a favorable condition to foster its success, resulting in Noah's story becoming a major prophetic truth in the tapestry of redemption. The patriarch's father, Lamech, named Noah whose name means "rest." God indeed permitted the entire creation to find rest in His agreement with Noah. The whole world was destroyed in a flood of God's unquestionable wrath, engendering the complete restoration of the earth by God's divine mandate.

Noah's father made a prognostic declaration at his birth found in Genesis 5:29, which reads, *"And he called his name Noah, saying, 'This one will comfort us concerning our work and the toil of our hands, because of the ground which the Lord has cursed.'"* In so doing, he released the express purpose of God upon the head of his son permitting a godly consequence. As we have covered in an earlier chapter concerning the covenant of the fathers, words spoken by patriarchs, particularly when orchestrated by the sovereign God, bear greater weight than those spoken by happenstance. That is why it is so critically imperative that we consider what we release in the realm of the Spirit over our children, our families, and if in ministry, our flocks. If we behave in poor character, our children will replicate our behavior. If we do what is right in the sight of the Lord, our children (spiritual and natural) will also follow that good habit. It is equally essential to comprehend our station in life and our stature in the spirit realm. At certain junctures of our existence, we are suffered more power and authority than at others. Noah's father vicariously passed this concept on to his son through the legacy found in his name. Because of this, Noah's covenant was, is and will be totally fulfilled.

Most ministers place great emphasis on the fact that Noah preached 120 years presumably unsuccessful in his endeavors. There are but a few who offer a reasonable explanation as to why or, better yet, what was ineffective! The fact of the matter is, Noah's generation had produced a wicked line of infiltration from the satanic kingdom that was more than remarkable. The Lord knew this would happen and had to prevent the inception of an even greater number of mutant giants who would eventually dominate world society. As it was, the preservation of Ham, Shem and Japheth, along with their spouses, permitted the birth of several others of these ogres the equivalent of Goliath *after* the flood.

However, with the Father, a holy contract is a holy contract. Because of this fact, He raised up righteous men to defeat evil giants who were also representatives of the principles espoused in Heaven. And so, while Noah's preaching did not gather a crowd on the ark, it was sufficient enough to appropriate the souls who could be approved of God, a sad testimony to the devoutness of that generation. Noah preached 120 years, the number of years to which God reduced man's life span - with stipulations. This was a sign of judgment executed, for the Lord allowed one year of preaching for every potential year of life promised for living right before Him. Presently, everyone is still given an opportunity to live this length of time. However, so few lived to see 120 years even directly after the flood, but it is possible to this day if we keep God's covenant. Science and technology are dramatically increasing the prospect of the average person living this duration of time.

This is Jehovah's adoration and grace given to us, and it is so undeserved. Please allow me to reiterate a serious fact: The Father could not send a righteous judgment without the word being released through the mouth of a prophet. Whether it was believed or not, the Lord refused to act without it. This keeps balance in the universe and gives Satan no room for argument. The sum of the matter is, Noah did not fail, although His contemporaries failed God miserably.

Many Old Testament stories were written both to record his dory and to define ideologies advocated by God above. The Father predicated the heart of His covenant upon blood both as light and fluid. God is pure light but cannot shine in His fullness toward us until our bodies are glorified and our minds are restored to the glory that was upon the original man, Adam. Until that day, we will have to content ourselves with enjoying light slowed down to become sound (sound giving us the prophetic word of the Lord), and then slowed down again to become the blood that courses through our veins.

It is the blood of Jesus that will propel us swiftly toward the pureness of the light that is God. This is why blood is required to remit sin, for without the shedding of blood there is no remission from sin. With the infiltration of wickedness in the bloodline of man, the Almighty was forced to find other means of accomplishing giving birth to a line of virtuous humans through which to send the Master in generations to come. Noah's generation simply could not have fulfilled that requirement. They were too close to the fall of Eden and its impious deposit against civilization.

After the flood it repented God that He had to perform such a feat. He made a promise to mankind that is really a guarantee or concurrence with Himself: God pledged He would never again destroy the world by water. The next time it would be by fire. Why water the first time? Because the world was framed through the constructive force of God's spoken Word. The washing of the water of the Word is what brings life to the iniquitous spirits of men. Fire is necessary for the final deliverance, for it thoroughly purges all things allowing nothing to stand in its present state. All must be reconstructed, even though the image of the former glory may be visible.

This is what happens to a converted soul: The fire of God cleanses and delivers and will continuously do so until everything is renewed. It is also representative of the Lord of Heaven's very nature. Jeremiah summed up a heavenly infiltration by the Father of spirits by exclaiming, "It was like fire shut up in my bones" (See Jeremiah 20:9 KJV). Hebrews 12:29 reinforces the summation of the matter: *"Our God is a consuming fire."* If we recognize and construct our Christian lives upon this premise, we will find no drought polluting our essence that would require Him to cleanse us by fire. You may choose to be consumed by the fire of God that devours and annihilates all wickedness or be born again and become a part of the flame. We should rather be ignited with His hallowed fire to do His service.

Chapter 10
The Covenant of Moses

Moses is a most intriguing figure as it pertains to covenant. His story is among the most famous of the Bible both to believers and nonbelievers alike. This figure was born in one of the most turbulent seasons for ancient Israel. In accordance with God's agreement with Abraham, Moses' birth was brought about for the distinct purpose of delivering the aberrant seed of the patriarch. His story begins with the intrepid, virtuous mother, Jochebed, assigning Miriam, his sister, to place baby Moses (not yet named in the Scripture), into a tightly woven, pitched straw basket, committing him to the tumultuous Nile River. Pharaoh had made a decree that all Hebrew baby boys between birth and three years of age were to be destroyed. When Jochebed could no longer hide her handsome child, she relegated his fate to the Nile and Jehovah. He drifted despite the churning of the waters until his straw craft rested itself at the feet of Pharaoh's very daughter.

When she ventured to open the lid, a cry emanated that transcended time and space, articulating the cry of nearly 450 years of bondage. There were practically four and a half million Jews held captive as slaves to Rameses I, Pharaoh of Egypt. His intention at this point was to build the greatest city ever on the bloody backs of Israel. They were a threat because of their size, and this king did not know Joseph with whom Egypt covenanted. Israel had legal rights to Egyptian land by that covenant, thus jeopardizing the inheritance of the sequential lineage of sons to the throne of Egypt. Moses, whose very name means "drawn out of water," became the living water of salvation to Israel, giving her the opportunity to drink freely and come into the fullness of her inheritance in God. It is sometimes of great benefit to be raised in the house of the oppressor to gain advantageous information as to how to turn the tide of oppression. Such was the case with Moses. He received an affluent education with the greatest of care at the feet of the monarch. His vast education aided him immensely in the understanding of his mission to Israel. In this an underlying principle of the Kingdom is exposed, and that is that God wastes nothing.

Sometimes the very things we considered dead to us are resurrected and presented for their true purpose in a season we never imagined would come upon us, and one in which we needed them the most. Through an extraordinary turn of events, the Father caused Moses to be told the truth about his nativity, and at age forty he sought his origins. Trouble was in fortune in this quest that ends with righteous indignation commanding him to slay an unruly taskmaster for unjustly thrashing a slave. When the thing was known, he fled his surrogate father's house to be raised for forty years in the exigent (demanding) house of his divine Father.

At age eighty, Moses meets providence in the flames of an unconsumed burning bush. The Father infuses His will and purpose upon the patriarch, and Israel's liberation from the tyranny of her subjugators is born. Now the leader is given clearly articulated orders as to how to discharge his commission. He is reintroduced to his natural family, and brother Aaron becomes his spokesman/prophet.
God takes Moses through a series of trials that bring him to a point of fearlessness. First, he is shown the awesomeness of God (in the burning bush experience), followed by the fear of God (in the smiting of his own flesh with leprosy), and then the determination of God to execute purpose (through the plagues). At this point Moses is armed with a new faith in a God he did not really know. He feels providence and is compelled to act upon its pronouncements.

In Exodus 5:1, the Lord sends a powerful directive to the Pharaoh of Egypt. Moses, the apostolic power of Israel, along with Aaron his prophet brother, takes the edict, *"Let My people go"* to Pharaoh. Pharaoh does not listen and causes God to show His hand to the fullest degree. The children of Israel, ten plagues later, leave

Egypt unharmed, healed and healthy, rich, feared and grateful. Currently, the Middle East and Africa are grave sources of upheaval for the world, for everything began there and everything not connected to God's Kingdom on earth will end there. This is a part of the covenant of Moses. Egypt is described as the cradle of civilization. It is thought to be the land of the Garden of Eden. Particularly pertinent is the fact that its rich history, both spiritual and natural, are grave reasons for this focus.

Egypt, according to the *International Standard Bible Encyclopedia,* "usually is supposed to represent the dual of 'Mitsrayim,' referring to 'the two lands,' as Egyptians call their country."[3] *The New Unger's Bible Dictionary* says of Egypt: "The ancient Egyptians were Hamitic peoples (Genesis 10:6). Later on an invasion from Babylonia, predominantly Semitic, came into the country and left its imprint upon the language and culture."[4] The religions of Egypt were polytheistic and contingent upon what the pharaoh of that day believed, he being a chief god.

Nelson's Illustrated Bible Dictionary says: The Egyptians were polytheists, believing in many gods. Many of these gods were the personification of nature, such as the Nile, the sun and the earth. But other gods stood for abstract concepts such as wisdom, justice, and order. The Egyptians believed that the gods were intimately involved with all aspects of life. The gods caused the rain, controlled the growth of crops, determined birth and death, and ultimately were behind everything. They did not give natural explanations to events, because they made no distinction between the secular and the sacred.

The Israelites also believed that God was the force behind everything, but they had only one God who was not identified with

---

[3] International Standard Bible Encyclopedia (Electronic Database by Biblesoft, 1996).
[4] The New Unger's Bible Dictionary (Chicago, IL: Moody Press, 1988).

any part of nature. The Egyptians confused the Creator with His creation. Many of these nature deities were represented as animals (bull, crocodile, falcon, ram, jackal) or by a part human and part animal statue. Since each god was the king of its own realm of influence, it was treated as a king in its temple. The deity would be awakened, washed, dressed, fed (by an offering), taken for walks and put to bed. (These practices were totally opposite to the activities in the Israelite Temple, where God was separated from the priest in the Holy of Holies.)

The Pharaoh himself was one of the most important Egyptian gods. While ruling, he was the incarnation of the god Horus and the son of Re. After his death, he was identified with the god Osiris. [We have adopted these same gods and dogmas in the practice of Freemasonry]. The Pharaoh was a mediator between the people and the cosmic gods of the universe. Thus, the Pharaoh was a key factor in determining the fate of the nation. The worship of Osiris was one of the most important aspects of Egyptian religion. Osiris was the king of the underworld, where people went after death, as well as the god of [male] fertility.[5]

The Plagues of Egypt

This sets us up for an inimitable look at the ten plagues. These are the ten plagues of Egypt according to *The New Unger's Bible Dictionary* and *The International Standard Bible Encyclopedia*.

1. **Blood**[6] – (Exodus 7:19-25). Pharaoh, having hardened his heart against the first sign, empowered Moses and Aaron to enforce the release of Israel by a series of punishing miracles .. The changing of the water into blood is to be interpreted in the same sense as in Joel 2:31, where the moon is said to be turned into blood; that is to say,

---

[5] Nelson's Illustrated Bible Dictionary (Thomas Nelson, Publishers, 1986).

[6] The New Unger's Bible Dictionary.

not as a chemical change into real blood, but as a change in the color, which caused it to assume the appearance of blood (2 Kings 3:22). The miracle was imitated by the magicians. This plague was humiliating, inasmuch as the Egyptians were so dependent upon the Nile for water that they worshiped it as a god, as well as some of its fish.

2. **Frogs**[7] – (Exodus 8:1-15). The second plague also proceeded from the Nile and consisted of unparalleled numbers of frogs. As foretold to Pharaoh, the frogs not only penetrated into the houses and inner rooms and crept into the domestic utensils, the beds, the ovens, and the kneading troughs, but they even got upon the men themselves. This miracle was also imitated by the Egyptian magicians, who made *"frogs come up on the land of Egypt"* (v. 7 NAS)... They could not remove the evil, for Pharaoh was obliged to send for Moses and Aaron to intercede with Jehovah to take them away. This request of Pharaoh, coupled with the promise to let the people go, was a sign that he regarded Jehovah as the author of the plague. This plague must have been aggravating to the Egyptians, for the frog was included among their sacred animals, in the second class of local objects of worship. It was sacred to the goddess Hekt, who is represented with the head of this animal.

3. **Gnats/lice**[8] – (Exodus 8:16-19). Gnats creep into the eyes and nose, and they have a sting that causes a painful irritation. The plague was caused by Aaron's smiting the dust of the ground with his staff; all the dust throughout the land of Egypt thereupon turned into gnats, which were upon man and beast. The failure of the magicians in this instance is believed to have been because of God's restraint of the demoniac powers.

---

[7] The New Unger's Bible Dictionary.
[8] The New Unger's Bible Dictionary.

4. **Flies**[9] – (Exodus 8:20). The increased severity of this plague, and the providential interference to separate between Israel and the Egyptians, drove Pharaoh and his people to such desperation that Pharaoh gave a half-guarantee of liberty for Israel to sacrifice "in the land." This called out the statement that they would sacrifice the "abomination of the Egyptians." This may have referred to the sacrifice of sheep, which were always held in more or less detestation by Egyptians, or it may have had reference to the sacrifice of heifers, the cow being the animal sacred to the goddess Hathor. [Keep in mind that Satan is the "lord of the flies."]

5. **Pestilence**[10] – (Exodus 9:1-7). This plague consisted of a severe disease that killed the cattle of the Egyptians that were in the field, those of the Israelites being spared. That the loss of cattle seems to have been confined to those in the field must be understood from verse 3 and from the fact that there were beasts to be killed by the hail (v. 25). Again, this plague was an insult to the gods of Egypt, for the cow, the calf and the bull were all worshiped there. The heart of Pharaoh still remained hardened.

6. **Boils**[11] – The sixth plague was of boils breaking forth in sores (Exodus 9:8-12). Moses and Aaron took soot or ashes from a smelting furnace or limekiln and threw it toward Heaven. This flew like dust throughout the land and became boils. The magicians appear to have tried to protect the king by their secret arts but were attacked themselves.

7. **Hail**[12] – (Exodus 9:17-35). In response to the continued hardness of Pharaoh, Jehovah determined to send such hail as had not been known since Egypt became a nation (vv. 18,24). A warning was sent out for all God-fearing Egyptians to house servants and cattle, thus

---

[9] The International Standard Bible Encyclopedia.
[10] The New Unger's Bible Dictionary.
[11] The New Unger's Bible Dictionary.
[12] The New Unger's Bible Dictionary.

showing the mercy of Jehovah. The hail was accompanied by thunder and lightning, the latter coming down like burning torches, and multitudes of men and beasts were slain, trees and plants destroyed. Terrified by the fierceness of the storm, Pharaoh called for Moses and Aaron and said, "I have sinned this time. The Lord is righteous and my people are wicked" (v. 27 NAS). Moses promised to pray to Jehovah on behalf of the Egyptians that the storm cease; but as soon as the storm ceased Pharaoh again hardened his heart and refused permission to Israel.... The havoc caused by this plague was greater than any of the earlier ones; it destroyed men, which others seem not to have done.

8. **Locusts**[13] – (Exodus 10:1-20). A compromise was suggested, by which the men should be allowed to go and wor-=ship, but that the women should remain... This compromise was rejected, and Moses and Aaron were driven from the king's presence. Moses lifted up his staff, and the Lord brought an east wind, which the next day brought locusts...They came in such dreadful swarms as Egypt had never known before, nor has experienced since. *"They covered the surface of the whole land, so that the land was darkened ..Thus nothing green was left on tree or plant of the field throughout all the land of Egypt"* (v. 15 NAS). The fact that the wind blew a day and a night before bringing up the locusts showed that they came from a great distance, and therefore proved to the Egyptians that the omnipotence of God reached far beyond the borders of Egypt and ruled over every land. In response to Pharaoh's entreaty the Lord *"shifted the wind to a very strong west wind which took up the locusts and drove them into the Red Sea..."* (v. 19 NAS).

9. **Darkness**[14] – (Exodus 10:21-29). As the king still continued to be defiant, a continuous darkness came over all Egypt, with the exception of Goshen (v. 23). It is described as a "thick darkness" (v.

---

[13] The New Unger's Bible Dictionary.

[14] The New Unger's Bible Dictionary.

22 NAs). Isaiah 60:2 KJV says: *"For, behold, the darkness shall cover the earth, and gross darkness the people: but the Lord shall arise upon thee, and his glory shall be seen upon thee."*

The combination of two words or synonyms gives the greatest intensity to the thought. The darkness was so great that they could not see one another, and no man rose from his place. The Israelites alone *"had light in their dwellings"* (v. 23 NAS). The darkness which covered the Egyptians, and the light which shone upon the Israelites were types of the wrath and grace of God. Again, the theology of Egypt was attacked; the sun god was blotted out by the thick darkness ... Pharaoh proposed another compromise, that the Israelites, men, women, and children, should go, but that the flocks and herds should remain. But Moses insisted upon the cattle being taken for the purpose of sacrifices and burnt offerings, saying, *"Not a hoof shall be left behind..."* (v. 26 NAS). This firmness Moses defended by saying, "We ourselves do not know with what we shall serve the Lord." At this Pharaoh was so enraged that he not only dismissed Moses but also threatened him with death if he should come into his presence again. Moses answered, *"You are right; I shall never see your face again!"* (v. 29 NAS). God had already told Moses that the last blow would be followed by the immediate release of the people, and there was no further necessity for him to appear before Pharaoh.

10. The final plague, the **death of the firstborn**[15] – (Exodus 11:1-12:30). The brief answer of Moses (10:29) was followed by an address (11:4-8) in which Moses announced the coming of the last plague and declared that *"there shall be a great cry in all the land of Egypt, such as there has not been before and such as shall never be again"* (v. 6 NAS), and that the servants of Pharaoh would come to Moses and entreat him to go with all the Israelites.

---

[15] The New Unger's Bible Dictionary.

Then Moses commanded the Israelites to ask from the Egyptians articles of silver and gold, and the Egyptians readily *"let them have their request"* (Exodus 12:36 NAS). The *Passover* was instituted, and the houses of the Israelites sprinkled with the blood of the lambs. The firstborn of the Egyptians were struck at <u>midnight</u>, as Moses had forewarned Pharaoh. The clearly miraculous nature of this plague, coming as it did without intervention on the part of Moses, taking only the firstborn, and sparing those of the Israelites, must have convinced Pharaoh that he had to deal with the One who inflicted this punishment by His own omnipotence. That very night Pharaoh sent for Moses and Aaron and gave them permission to depart with their people, their children, and their cattle, even urging haste.

Moses and Aaron presented themselves to Pharaoh and God plagued Egypt because of the hardness of Pharaoh's heart. He simply did not want to let the children of Abraham go, but God would not permit Himself to be released from His pledge to Abraham. This forced Pharaoh's hand. Each unique plague represented a ruling prince of darkness worshiped at the time by Egypt, including Pharaoh. God smote the land, its cattle, crops, people, and lastly, firstborn sons, mimicking the law of reciprocity. Because they killed Israel's sons, God smote theirs (the firstborn of any of Israel's creatures was considered holy before the Lord because of the fall of Adam). When all the relentless verdicts were rendered, Israel once again was released only to have Pharaoh pursue them for the last time. He and the host of his warriors were drowned in the Red Sea, ending centuries of repression and thwarted aspirations.

Moses' story is quite prolific in that the Lord fulfilled a major patriarchal covenant (Abraham's) to bring Israel's chief minister to the fulfillment of his destiny. To begin with, God alludes to Satan's deceitful sin in Heaven of trafficking. Trade, commerce and economy are a major part of the rulership of any nation, including Heaven. While it is not essential that we be given the exact details of his trade and commerce in Heaven, it is imperative to grasp that he was ousted from his place in the heavenly kingdom for violating a premise in relation to it. When God spoiled Egypt, the final blow was the taking of the workforce. This caused her economy to crumble, taking years to recover. That same mighty workforce was transplanted from a land of torment to a virtual Valhalla, a land opulent in wealth and resources.

Ezekiel 28:18 says:

You defiled your sanctuaries by the multitude of your iniquities, by the iniquity of your trading [trafficking: merchandise, commerce, trade]; **therefore I brought fire from your midst; it devoured you, and I turned you to ashes upon the earth in the sight of all who saw you.** Jehovah is a wise ruler and determined that in order to undo the nation and justly ratify His covenant with Israel's father, He would need to ruin the economy. It is most difficult at best to pursue four and a half million people if you have no wherewithal by which to pursue them! Further, the *destruction* of Egypt was necessary to the *construction* of the new Israel. God's economy is not the same as ours. Whenever He transitions from one move to another, the economy of the former movement is diminished because He must transfer the wealth to the present move. So it was with Pharaoh and the old order. Israel had to be free of all of the systems of Egypt in order to function under the new order of the Kingdom of Heaven.

God cut a covenant with Abraham in Genesis, chapter 15, with residual effects spanning every generation from that time to this. He gave Israel's ancient father the assurance of possessing the land spoken of in Genesis 15:19-21, inhabited by the Kenites, Kenizzites, Kadmonites, Hittites, Perizzites, Rephaims, Amorites, Canaanites, Girgashites, and the Jebusites. This choice land was the richest in the known world. If this relevant factor were imputed to God, coupled with the brilliant addition of a workforce, the director could create a utopia as close to Eden as possible on the outward side of its guardian cherubim.

Moses was chosen to be the leader that brought them to the entrance of the new empire. However, sin and a unique breach of accord brought the extraordinary leader to the brink of only tasting total victory alone. He was not permitted to lead the people. but was replaced by Joshua (his name is a form of Yeshua, which means "salvation"), a loyal warrior of God's crown. Many argue that God made a vow to the apostle, Moses, that would see the fruition of Israel's inheritance in his lifetime. God did make the promise to Moses and Aaron that they would lead the children of Israel into the promised land, for God cannot lie. The disheartening truth is, these two patricians contravened the Lord at the waters of Meribah the second wine to such an extent that He could not permit them to cross over. One act of non-contrition caused an innovatory decision to be authorized from Heaven and the two dignitaries missed the promise long awaited.

Their first visit to Meribah ended well. Exodus 17:7 says, *"So he called the name of the place Massah and Meribah, because of the contention of the children of Israel, and because they tempted the Lord, saying, 'Is the Lord among us or not?"* The second was a fate-filled disaster. Numbers 20:10-11 says, *"And Moses and Aaron gathered the assembly together before the rock; and he said to them, 'Hear now, you rebels! Must we bring water for you out of this rock?' Then Moses lifted his hand and struck the rock twice with his rod; and water came out abundantly, and the congregation and their animals drank."* "Meribah" means contention, and "Massah" means temptation. Wherever there is contention and temptation, an egregious possibility threatens to breach covenant.

Herein lie the tender and sure mercies of God in that He always honors His covenant and keeps His Word even if we do not. The Word came to Moses that he would lead his people into a land "flowing with milk and honey." *The International Standard Bible Encyclopedia* defines "milk and honey" as: "Milk" is figuratively the word used (1) of abundance (Genesis 49:12); (2) of a loved one's charms (Song of Solomon 4:11); (3) of blessings (Isaiah 55:1; Joel 3:18); (4) of the (spiritual) food of immature people (1 Corinthians 3:2; Hebrews 5:12-13); (5) of purity (1 Peter 2:2). "Honey," figuratively: "A land flowing with milk and honey" suggested a land filled with abundance of good things (Exodus 3:8,17; Leviticus 20:24; Numbers 13:27; Deuteronomy 6:3; Joshua 5:6). "A land of olive trees and honey" had the same meaning (Deuteronomy 8:8; 2 Kings 18:32), and similarly "streams of honey and butter" (Job 20:17). Honey was a standard of sweetness (Song of Solomon 4: 11; Ezekiel 3:3; Revelation 10:9-10).

It typified sumptuous fare (Song of Solomon 5:1; Isaiah 7:15,22; Ezekiel 16:13,19). The ordinances of Yahweh were "sweeter than honey and the droppings of the honeycomb" (Psalms 19:10; 119:103). *"Thou didst eat...honey..."* (Ezekiel 16:13 KJV) expressed Yahweh's goodness to Jerusalem.[16] This land of milk and honey in definition was thoroughly exemplified in the prophetic overtones of all it held for Israel. Moses and Aaron did lead them to the promised land, and Moses was permitted as the chief leader to see the fulfillment of all his passion *in* the promised land at the Mount of Transfiguration. We who study the Word are aware of the fact that God keeps His Word. Moses, the lawgiver, was assuredly permitted to go into the promised land, only not with his beloved Israel but after his death. He broke the entire premise of the law of God in one willful act at Meribah. This progression to disobedience did not happen overnight but gradually and progressively.

So it is the same with all revolutions in leadership. Up until the point of insurgence, Moses had obeyed God in all things defending Israel to the brink of putting his own life on the line for

---

[16] The International Standard Bible Encyclopedia.

them. Their leaven had finally found a place in his heart, proving that the body can only be as strong as its head. It can be conjectured that Moses took the command of God that said He would make him as a *"God to Pharaoh"* (Exodus 7:1), and extended it to Israel also. He dared place himself in the place of God and he did so after writing the first commandment to have no other gods before Jehovah. God commanded him to speak to the rock the second time, but he smote the rock instead, and that twice! The defiance did not glorify God before an already rebellious people. Further, an insubordinate, fed-up and beleaguered ruler could only supplement the mutiny against God in the new nation. God at least leveled the playing field by giving them new leadership and direction along with the admonishment by the deaths of Moses and Aaron to comply in all things. In essence, Jehovah's answer was to allow the "rock," so to speak, to become a stone of stumbling for rebels.

First Peter 2:8 states, *"A stone of stumbling and a rock of offense." "They stumble, being disobedient to the word, to which they also were appointed."* Luke 20:18 says, *"Whoever falls on that stone will be broken; but on whomever it falls, it will grind him to powder."* Moses' "heart" was broken by the Father's corrective hand, which gained him access to future gratification at the Transfiguration. In that brief interlude in eternity, Moses' covenant was totally instituted.

The great Prophet Elijah, enforcer of the rule and law of God, pre-New Testament apostle and second man to cheat death before Christ, appeared to Jesus along with Moses before His absolute passion. This gallant prophet was translated by a fiery celestial chariot (possibly seraphim aflame with the fire of Heaven) into the presence of Yahweh. Because of this he could encourage the Christ, that God would also translate Him into glory after being victorious over death. Elijah in a sense had conquered death by not acquiescing to its grasp. Further, Malachi prophesied that Elijah would come before the great and terrible day of the Lord. John came in the "spirit of Elijah," but Elijah came to comfort the Lord that He would become the restorer of the breach, literally returning the hearts of the fathers to their children, and the hearts of the children to their fathers, preempting the necessity to strike the earth with a curse.

Moses too was a victor over death, for through death he was able to show the hand of God in a resurrection. Jesus satisfied both positions through His undertaking. Moses was laid to rest by God Himself, his fatal frame hidden from the peering eyes of darkness only to be resurrected at the appointed time to give succor and counsel to the law's fulfiller. Jesus was laid to rest by men, only to conquer death before the peering eyes of demons by the resurrection of God!

Elijah proclaimed the law, enforced it, committed extraordinary miracles to it, pressed governments to follow it, and was transmitted by it into glory. Moses wrote it, was governed by it, had a face-to-face encounter with God behind it and died through its piousness. The lawgiver who died met the lawkeeper who was translated over the form of the glorified Christ who certified it by uniting both factions on the Mount of Transfiguration. Jesus was now preparing to be debased in the place of the people for its aim, surrendering all to the will of His Father, causing eternity to further empower the Mosaic covenant through Calvary. No other counsel would be fitting and found worthy of this task than these assigned to the commission before time began. In Christ's atonement, all of the failures of the law and its writer were turned to awe-inspiring, glorious victory. God's purpose for the law can now reign supreme among men, for it is inscribed upon the heart. This is the power of the Master's redeeming grace and diligence to discharge every iota of His spoken words of covenant.

Chapter 11
The Covenant of David

Although King David was not the first king of Israel, God uniquely professed him to be the first after His heart and mind. God presented David as prophet, priest and king, but the Lord's objective was for Israel to accept Him as their king exclusively. This was not to be, for Israel demanded of the Great King the substitution of a natural king. God's order is excellent. Therefore, He would have provided them with exceptional leadership had they not made the demand. His paramount objective was to place into position apostolic and prophetic rulers who could govern, administrate and enforce the plan of God according to His expressed will. This is the literal order that is now being re-established in the church today. When the order was violated, Jehovah gave them a man after their own hearts first, and secondarily, a man after His heart.

Men like David were rare in that day. He was anointed, God-fearing, young, malleable and strong in conviction — entirely what the nation needed from God. He was handsome and earthy but not bawdy or outrageous. In short, he was a prince with a divinely assigned Kingdom. As a shepherd David spent massive amounts of time in the wilderness alone, facing its perils under the same circumstance alone. He feared little and relied on his Heavenly Father for everything. Anyone God ordains for covenant passes His stringent qualifications to obtain authoritative positioning in it. They all have one major thing in common: Each will have a wilderness experience, and each will be forced to submit to the process in the wilderness.

David's wilderness experience was two-fold: one as a shepherd, the other as a soldier. A wilderness does not have to be barren, for his proved to be quite fruitful. In the first experience he learned how to keep the flocks of God and how to defeat insurmountable obstacles while keeping the sheep satisfied. A lion and a bear were not easy to subdue. In order to defeat a lion he needed his qualities of brute strength, endurance, intelligence (almost crafty), and survival skills. All of this was necessary for him to endure a kingship with the likes of ancient Israel! The same qualities were needful to survive the ravages of the bear; only his qualities took in digesting the bitter with the sweet. David excelled and prevailed over them both.

David's second wilderness experience was the most intricate. Whereas the first instructed him in how to keep and defend God's flocks, the second taught him how to subject himself to God-appointed authorities, even when they are as corrupt and envious as Saul. He learned wisdom and fortitude beyond what he could imagine. An essential lesson in all of this was the erudition (intense learning) of how to do things properly as opposed to improperly. Until you have been chased down by your "Saul," you will never know true humility and fervent endurance, coupled with the reserve to continue against all odds. This was David's most vital lesson of all. After returning from this wilderness, he was thoroughly equipped for his kingly mission.

This kind of remarkable experience is not at all uncharacteristic of the life of one called to a high position in God's Kingdom. All great apostles and prophets of the covenant find themselves in strange, intricate trials that temper them, bringing the subject to a place of serene surrender to the Lord. Otherwise we will not be fit to be a spokesman for the Almighty. It is after these stringent tests that we ascend to greatness, acknowledging His sufferings that bring wealth to all our endeavors. As arduous as it may seem, we truly would not trade these ordeals for anything. They become the platform for our greatness and the anchor for our faith. The anointing of David by Samuel the prophet was as dramatic as any occasion of covenant ever. Normally this kind of anointing could only be performed after an animal had been sacrificed, but this was not the case with David's first ordination to kingship. The Heavenly Father knew that David would soon give birth to **the sacrifice**, the Lamb of God.

First Samuel 16:10-13, speaking of David's anointing, says: **Thus Jesse made seven of his sons pass before Samuel. And Samuel said to Jesse, "The Lord has not chosen these?" And Samuel said to Jesse, "Are all the young men here?" Then he said, "There remains yet the youngest, and there he is, keeping the sheep? And Samuel said to Jesse, "Send and bring him. For we will not sit down till he comes here." So he sent and brought him in. Now he was ruddy, with bright eyes, and good-looking. And the Lord said, "Arise, anoint him; for this is the one!' Then Samuel took the horn of oil and anointed him in the midst of his brothers; and the Spirit of the Lord came upon David from that day forward. So Samuel arose and went to Ramah.**

David was anointed and appointed to the task from that day onward. Notice that David did nothing of his own accord to see to it that the agreement between he and God would come to pass. It was up to the Lord to arrange the circumstances of its performance. David's stellar opportunity offered itself in the form of Jesse's (his father's) need to send provisions to his sons on the battlefield. Upon arrival David observed the Israeli army cowering from its enemy (their king hiding behind his own importance and bureaucracy), the Philistines, and their 11-to-13-foot champion Goliath. His humiliated brother chastised him for asking why they fled. David then spoke these providential words: *"Is there not a cause?"* (1 Samuel 17:29). His inquiry was that of a nobleman and warrior. It was not a question of, "Is there a reason for this alone?" but a bold statement of, "Why would one flee the likes of Goliath!"

He was ushered before King Saul who promptly displayed his lack of understanding as a commander by offering David his armor. David tries it, thanks the king, but refuses it, for he saw the giant through another light, the light of covenant. The youngest son of Jesse realized that it was not by might, nor by power, but by the Spirit of the Lord that he would become the victor. Saul's armor was too weighty for a boy. The boy had to grow into kingship, and above all, by God's standards. Far too many people attempt to wear the armor of the days ahead prematurely and fall to the weight of it. David did not succumb to this temptation.

God's plan required him to be swift and light on his feet. He had slain the lion and the bear, which were creatures of the covenant of creation. An uncircumcised man was no foe to a man of the covenant of Jehovah despite his arcane size. Had he retained the protective covering, David would have been hindered from running up on his enemy and would be forced to move at a slower pace. He would not be able to avoid the grasp of the giant. The real issue was not to protect himself from Goliath but rather to cause Goliath to be in a disadvantageous position! This strategy had already been proven a winner with a lion and a bear. It is all in how you view it.

Archbishop Veron Ashe of the Syrian Orthodox Church of Fresno, California, while preaching concerning David and Goliath, gave this powerful insight. His Eminence said that Goliath (whose name means "soothsayer"), a Philistine (which means "strange things"), was attired in the heaviest of metals, held a shield too cumbersome to wield, had a spear that was immense and top heavy (rendering it impossible to be thrown in a straight line), and wore footing that was absurd. The giant was described as everything but a warrior for he wasn't. He was an illusionist causing one to think he was powerful, but if he really was required to do combat he could not move around to do battle for he was too encumbered. The entire fallacy of Goliath was based upon the mirage of intimidation. He could not fight. Therefore, the illusion was created to cause his enemies to be intimidated by his size. He was a bluffer. Israel said Goliath was too big to prevail over. *David said he was too big to miss!*

The eyes of covenant know the victory is assured, especially when you consider that the anointing must fight against a huge, "strange soothsayer!" David knew he had a divine appointment with destiny. His accord with the "Father of accords" was massive. We must adopt his very attitude of knowing we have won before the battle ensues, or in the least, believe that winning is possible in the Lord, in order to be triumphant in all of our pursuits. These two passages of Scripture tell the account of David's covenant. They are Second Samuel 7 and First Kings 9.

> *Now therefore, thus shall you say to My servant David, "Thus says the Lord of hosts: 'I took you from the sheepfold, from following the sheep, to be ruler over My people, over Israel. And I have been with you wherever you have gone, and have cut off all your enemies from before you, and have made you a great name, like the name of the great men who are on the earth. Moreover I will appoint a place for My people Israel, and will plant them, that they may dwell in a place of their own and move no more; nor shall the sons of wickedness oppress them anymore, as previously, Since the time that I commanded judges to be over My people Israel, and have caused you to rest from all your enemies. Also the Lord tells you that He will make you a house. When your days are fulfilled and you rest with your fathers, I will set up your seed after you, who will come from your body, and I will establish his kingdom.'" 2 Samuel 7:8-12*

> *Then I will establish the throne of your kingdom over Israel forever [speaking of Solomon], as I promised David your father, saying, "You shall not fail to have a man on the throne of Israel." 1 Kings 9:5*

So requisite was the agreement that Jesus was called "the son of David," and "the root and offspring of David." David was a brilliant military leader and left an extraordinarily substantial kingdom behind. He was a devout worshiper and psalmist skilled in a stringed instrument, and among the greatest supporters of the priesthood of Israel. David was always honest to God, even when wrong. He prayed the heart of God, which was oftentimes his own heart also.

However, this *earthly* king was not permitted to build the Lord an *earthly* tabernacle because he had blood on his hands. The assumption that the privilege was denied because David was a man of war is in error if you comprehend God's covenant agreement with this father of kings. David was anointed to advance the Kingdom as a man of war. In Second Samuel 11, David commits a grievous sin against Jehovah. The Bible articulated that in the spring, at the time when kings go off to war, David was on his roof instead of on the battlefield of kings. We are warned, "Woe unto them that are at ease in Zion!" He spied a beautiful young black woman who was married to one of the most loyal soldiers in all of David's army, Uriah the Hittite. He bid her come to the palace for reasons she knew not of. Many scholars have tarnished the reputation of Bathsheba by assuming her to be a seductress. This supposition is purely based upon the information that is presented that says she was on the roof bathing, probably with her maids.

In order to make a judgment of the reason for Bathsheba being introduced into the story of the first God-breathed king of Israel, we must examine the history of the moment in order to keep things in perspective. To begin with, Israel and the surrounding areas were at war. The *kings* were at war, but King David was at home. Women, during the time of menses, were considered ceremonially unclean until seven days into the cycle or until the bleeding ceased. Anything she sat on was thought to be unclean by the law and anyone who touched those things she sat on had to wash their clothing and bathe. This would be one reason for her being outside of her home and bathing. The Bible said that when David sent for her, he lay with her and makes note of the fact that *she had been purified from her uncleanness.* (This would also explain why she was vulnerable to pregnancy, and why the king would not hesitate to have intercourse with her. She was ceremonially clean).

It would be dangerous for her to proceed to an isolated place outside her compound during a war. There was a tradition that a certain flag flew from the castle to let Israel know that the king was in residence. However, in times of war the flag would not fly because it would alert the enemy as to the whereabouts of the king. The Bible does not make it clear (but only implies) as to why she was bathing on the roof, but it also, in my estimation, does not make it clear that she did it to seduce the king. This woman had no idea why the king would bid her come but was under mandate of law to obey the dictates of the monarch without question.

The other side of the argument is that in a closed society, such as the military community of Israel, all of the military families would be aware of the king being in residence. Were that true, this woman could have potentially known that King David was indeed in residence and also in eyeshot of her roof. When the Lord sent the Prophet Nathan to render the verdict upon David, Bathsheba was not mentioned as being at fault, but only David. The analogy in the prophecy referred to her being the equivalent of one delicate ewe lamb in the hands of a man who adored it, being taken from her tender, loving shepherd's watch care by one who had flocks and a potential for gaining more flocks beside.

I learned from the Jewish people that the paschal lamb that was to be sacrificed during the Passover had to be like a member of the household. The Law said it must be a yearling. The Jews said that they treated it like a pet, feeding it under the household table and allowing it to live in the house with them for that year. This would cause the death of the dear animal to be even more meaningful, for the family was called to sacrifice a precious thing, the same way God was called to sacrifice the most precious thing in the universe to Him, His Son. Every practicing Jew would understand the symbolism in the story that Nathan told, and especially King David. God rebuked David as a man who could have had anything from Him that he desired, but instead he took the one prized possession of another man.

Even more essential is the fact that David was the father of all future kings in Israel by the command and concurrence of God. When he did not observe the law with integrity, he released a dangerous spirit of rebellion upon his seed. For God to compare Bathsheba's situation with that of a sacrificial lamb purported far more than most might think. God was saying that there would be a sacrifice demanded from David's line, but that he in return as a covenant father of Messiah could not require a sacrifice of a faithful follower like Uriah. He literally took from Uriah all that he had, for he took his wife and the man's life.

Bathsheba's story was to show the ravages of sin, particularly sexual sin. When David sent for her and lay with her, he sired a child. When David could not get his faithful servant to go lay with his wife (so as to cause it to appear that he sired the child), this great sin caused David to conspire to have her husband placed in the heat of the fray so as to insure his death. The desperate plot succeeded and the king quickly married the ill-gotten widow. This shameful transgression cost him and her their firstborn son and peaceful succession of his children to the throne. Bloodguiltiness caused him not to be able to build the permanent temple for the Lord. David was called as a man of war and had he been abiding in his calling the fateful day he was on the roof, his covenant would never have been fraught with disaster.

The results of breaching covenant with God can be noxious! For David it took the form of the death of his firstborn son, the rebellion and consequent murder of his beloved son, Absalom, the death of tens of thousands of Israelites after his legendary numbering of the troops, the sword never departing from his kingdom for long, and the roots of rebellion transcending to many of his sons who would occupy the throne to this day. For her, the mention of her name was eliminated from the lineage of Christ, not to mention the loss of a child and a faithful husband. Even Solomon, the wisest king to live and David's chosen heir, rebelled against God with foreign gods from relationships with foreign wives.

Solomon became king for two important reasons: God upheld His covenant with David and Bathsheba was honored for her lack of choice in being taken by the king. Her name was not mentioned in the lineage of Christ, in my estimation, because God did not recognize the union of David and Bathsheba in respect to His Son of the covenant. Instead, God addresses her in Matthew 1:6 as *"her who had been the wife of Uriah,"* and not *the wife of David*. Solomon was blessed and highly favored of God as long as he kept God's covenant, proving the fact that God does not look at children as being illegitimate but at their parents when the children are conceived in a wrongful manner. David abused his kingly rights with Bathsheba, and all Israel, along with his ill-fated wife, suffered dearly because of it.

The intensity of David's covenant and the magnitude of his dominion, both in the earth and in the spirit, marked the intensity of both his punishment and triumph. David's covenant began with God's choice of a king for His chosen, Israel. Even though his older brothers towered over him giving a more kingly appearance, David's heart attracted the Lord who made him a choice over the preference of men. Our Heavenly Father never backs away from His choice, yet He loves us enough to permit us to choose to obey.

From the moment Samuel poured the horn of oil on David's head, the Almighty sealed his covenant. God made a vow to David that his seed would occupy the throne of Israel forever. This was a direct allusion to Messiah coming from the loins of the first God-chosen king of Israel. Second Samuel 7:11-16 confirms this agreement through the mouth of the Prophet Nathan, saying the Lord will ensure His covenant with the house of David. When David sleeps with his fathers, the Lord will raise up his son Solomon to sit upon his throne. When David's son(s) did wickedly, God promised to punish them but swore His allegiance to cause a son of David to remain on the throne of Israel perpetually.

God remained true to His Word as is exemplified in First Chronicles 28:3-5. He also reinforces His Word through the mouth of Jeremiah the prophet by saying, *"If you can break My covenant with the day and My covenant with the night, so that there will not be day and night in their season, then My covenant may also be broken with David My servant..."* (Jeremiah 33:20-21). The most revealing scriptural definition to this most critical covenant is found in the Psalms. God Almighty not only says whom He chose, but explains why He chose him and what His intentions were for all eternity. Psalm 89:19-38 proclaims:

"Then You spoke in a vision to Your holy one, and said: "I have given help to one who is mighty; I have exalted one chosen from the people. I have found My servant David; with My holy oil I have anointed him, with whom My hand shall be established; also My arm shall strengthen him. The enemy shall not outwit him, nor the son of wickedness afflict him. I will beat down his foes before his face, and plague those who hate him. But My faithfulness and My mercy shall be with him, and in My name his horn shall be exalted. Also I will set his hand over the sea, and his right hand over the rivers. He shall cry to Me, 'You are my Father, My God, and the rock of my salvation.' Also I will make him My firstborn, the highest of the kings of the earth. My mercy I will keep for him forever, and My covenant shall stand firm with him. His seed also I will make to endure forever, and his throne as the days of heaven. If his sons forsake My law and do not walk in My judgments, if they break My statutes and do not keep My commandments, then I will punish their transgression with the rod, and their iniquity with stripes. Nevertheless My

lovingkindness I will not utterly take from him, nor allow My faithfulness to fail. My covenant I will not break, nor alter the word that has gone out of My lips. Once I have sworn by My holiness; I will not lie to David: His seed shall endure forever and his throne as the sun before Me; it shall be established forever like the moon, even like the faithful witness in the sky." Selah.

So strong was David's relationship to Jehovah that he saw Jesus' passion on Calvary and wrote about it in Psalm 22. God knew that He could count on David to perpetuate His truth, causing David to become a keystone in the covenant of Christ. He is cited in the genealogy of Matthew, chapter 1. King David was a brilliant commander and military strategist, consummate orator and psalmist, dedicated worshipper and lover of God. With all of his imperfections, he was still immortalized as the man after God's own heart.

And when He had removed him, He raised up for them David as king, to whom also He gave testimony and said, "I have found David the son of Jesse, a man after My own heart, who will do all My will. Acts 13:22-23

Chapter 12
An Ancient Blood Covenant

At the onset of this book, it was agreed that most major covenants historically were codified, approved and/or sealed with an agreement wrought in blood. When the Father brought about a covenant with Abraham, He set the stage for the eternal covenant to be sanctioned through the sacrifice of Christ. This ethereal agreement would bring the joyous redemption so long awaited since the emergence of sin. Let us explore Abraham's covenant in light of a primordial Middle Eastern covenant that perhaps fashioned the rudimentary guidelines of the covenant of Abraham.

Articles of Covenant

There were eight articles of covenant in this old, pre-Judaic treatise. These articles are still relevant to the understanding of the full agreement between God and man given by Jesus to man.

1. The covenant partners knew each other very well. They may have been friends, neighbors or families conjoining the marriage of their children, business associates, co-ministries or missions, etc. Whatever the relationship, they enjoyed love and much respect for each other.

2. The covenant partners held all things as common. Properties were joint-owned as well as business pursuits and other entities. This insured the partners that there would be no lack. They exchanged or held common all of their earthly possessions even to their inheritances. This kind of judicious contract was seldom if ever abused or taken for granted.
3. The covenant was always presented before faithful witnesses.

4. Concluding the actual formulating of the agreement, the colleagues made certain exchanges with each other.

    a. The covenant partners exchanged robes or outer garments. This indicated the taking on of the identity of the other.

    b. They traded belts or girdles saying that they bound themselves to the cause of the other for life.

    c. They exchanged weapons of warfare that were fitly fastened to the belts. This signified spiritually and naturally that the bearer made a declaration before all men that the enemies of the partner are now his enemies and his family's for life. Of even greater consequence is the fact that the vow assured the protection of the partner and his family or assigns even if the defense of one partner resulted in the death of the other. The Bible says in John 15:13, *"Greater love has no one than this, than to lay down one's life for his friends."* This exchange also represented a binding together or oneness.

5. They offered an animal for sacrifice on an altar or in a field. The animal of choice was generally a bull, a lamb, a ram, turtledoves, etc. Family members, servants and others generally witnessed the covenant being contracted. The animal was cut across the throat and then down the center from stem to stern mirroring the cross. The sacrificed animal was laid on the ground after the giving of thanks to God or a lesser deity or, in some instances, a man. The sacrifice was divided apart upon the ground, leaving a wide enough space for the candidates to walk through. As the blood oozed through the center of the carcass(es), the partners walked what was called the "walk of death" through the pieces in a figure eight articulating to the witnesses their heartfelt oath of demanding God do the same to them and more if they or any of their assigns break the covenant.

After this, the partners carefully cut the right wrist, rubbed them together and mingled their blood. This cried out to all principalities of the spirit world that these covenant representatives were saying to each other, "We are now of one blood. May only death part us from the obligation of this covenant." The right hand indicated power and authority displaying an incessant fervor to keep unity for the sake of peace and submission to a deity. Unity begets strength. At the conclusion or when this transcendent feat was consummated, the partners referred to each other as friends.

To designate one as a friend in the truest sense was to identify that one as a covenant partner for life. God referred to us first as friend. James 2:23 says, *"Abraham believed God, and it was accounted to him for righteousness. And he was called the friend of God."*

6. The comrades exchanged last names in an analogous manner to western civilization. An excellent example would be some of the hyphenated names of the Bible, such as Simon bar-Jonas. The hyphen signified the bearer was of the house of Jonas, concluding the fact that a covenant had been ratified somewhere along the line whether by marriage or blood oath. When I married, I made a covenant with the house of Vinnett that included the house of Green. As is customary in the western civilization, I took the last name of my husband.

7. Bread and wine were considered a staple of the Israeli diet during the period this kind of covenant was common. The participants considered it fitting to indulge in a meal using bread and wine as a means by which to seal the covenant. In so doing, both parties assayed that each was now "flesh of my flesh and bone of my bone." In Genesis 14:18-20, *the king of Salem demonstrated the use of bread and wine as a conclusion to a treaty. "Then Melchizedek king of Salem brought out bread and wine; he was the priest of God Most High. And he blessed him and said: 'Blessed be Abram of God Most High, Possessor of heaven and earth; and blessed he God Most High, who has delivered your enemies into your hand.'"* This act of covenant was so strong that the Bible reports that Levi was in Abram's loins when the tithe (given to priests) was given to Melchizedek.

8. The final act of accord was the planting of a tree or the building of a sacred altar to mark the place of the covenant's empowerment. To show the veracity of this type of covenant, Jonathan and David exhibited several of these articles in First Samuel 18:1-4. *"The soul of Jonathan was knit to **the soul of David, and Jonathan loved him as his own soul**. Saul took him that day, and would not let him go home to his father's house anymore. Then **Jonathan and David made a covenant**, because he loved him as his own soul. And Jonathan **took off the robe** that was on him and **gave it to David, with his armor**, even to his **sword** and his **bow** and his **belt**."*

First Samuel 20:16 further supports the strength of this covenant. *"So Jonathan made a covenant with the house of David, saying, 'Let the Lord require it at the hand of David's enemies.'"* Notice that the transference of objects between Jonathan and David are exactly like or remarkably similar to the exchanges listed previously. As a result of this covenant, David looked for someone upon whom to bestow the riches of Jonathan's inheritance after his death. He chose Jonathan's son, Mephibosheth, who, from the point of his discovery, was granted the privilege of dining at the king's table for the remainder of his days (2 Samuel 9:6-13).

Saul thoroughly understood the potency of this covenant and destroyed the lives of the priests at Nob because of it. He berated the soldiers with fury as is revealed in First Samuel 22:8 – *"All of you have conspired against me, and there is no one who reveals to me that my son has made a covenant with the son of Jesse; and there is not one of you who is sorry for me or reveals to me that my son has stirred up my servant against me, to lie in wait, as it is this day."*

What sparked this antipathy? Saul knew that such an agreement would cause him to be coupled with his enemy, an infuriating thought. Nonetheless, this narrative supports the amalgamation of this early covenant into the fabric of the Jewish society of that day. Abraham's covenant (delineated in the chapter titled "The Covenants of Abraham and Noah") also exhibited certain characteristic points of this particular covenant. The sacrifice of the animal, the laying of the pieces on the ground and the "smoking furnace and burning lamp" (old *King James*) that performed the walk of death over the body of Abraham in the midst of those pieces. God agreed to this covenant by agreeing with Himself over the body of the seemingly dead prophet.

The Spiritual Significance of the Ancient Covenant

Each of the articles of this covenant bears substantial credence to our relationship with Christ due to His sacrifice. Upon examination, it is an excellent illustration of our Kingdom rights.

1. The covenant partners knew each other well. God knew and cherished us before the foundation of the world. His love for us was so thorough that His only begotten Son agreed to come to earth and save us before the beginning of time (2 Timothy 1:9). We are His plan and His vision, and for this reason He redeemed us.

2. Each constituent went into joint ownership. With us we were the recipients of the greater end of the indenture. Luke 12:32 says, *"Do not fear, little flock, for it is your Father's good pleasure to give you the kingdom."* We renounced sin, gave Him our sicknesses and sorrows and received the Kingdom. What a marvelous trade.

3. The covenant agreement was witnessed. When we repent and receive Jesus, the scripture says in Luke 15:10, *"Likewise, I say to you, there is joy in the presence of the angels of God over one sinner who repents."* Romans 8:16 says, *"The Spirit Himself bears witness with our spirit that we are children of God."* We are also admonished to be His witnesses by propitiating the gospel around the world.

4. The interchanges are made and in them we receive a helmet, breastplate, sword, girdle, shoes and shield (Ephesians 6:10-11). The Father totally equips us for the grueling battles ahead. We in return

give over our carnal thinking of warfare and enlist His aid as to how to win each battle. We also receive a splendid robe of righteousness in the place of our "filthy rags of sin." This clothes us in the identity of a son of God. The girding of salvation is our strong suit. Now His strength is made perfect in our weakness. Our enemies are now His enemies and vice versa. We should abhor sin just as our Father does, abstaining from it at all costs. It is our greatest enemy.

5. The ultimate blood sacrifice was made, and that is the blood of His dear Son. Christ's blood was shed once for the contrition of all men. Never again will the blood of an innocent animal be shed to pardon sin, for Jesus' body was broken as the paschal lamb. Now we need not be broken with sin, sickness or disease for Someone paid the crucial price for us. He puts to flight the seditious forces that work against us. We are absolved from having to take the interminable walk of death because the pardoned walk brings eternal life. We are able to die to selfishness and live as Christ. *"Therefore purge out the old leaven, that you may be a new lump, since you truly are unleavened. For indeed Christ, our Passover, was sacrificed for us"* (1 Corinthians 5:7).

6. God has given us a new name. For our everlasting purpose we will be known as Christians or saints here on earth and enduring sons in Heaven. We take on His identity. This accord should not be taken frivolously. You have been adopted into a family as a joint-heir with Christ, which factor grants a substantial responsibility. Walk in the fullness of that truth and honor His sacrifice, never rendering shame for His priceless gift. Hebrews 10:29 says, *"Of how much worse punishment, do you suppose, will he be thought worthy who has trampled the Son of God underfoot, counted the blood of the covenant by which he was sanctified a common thing, and insulted the Spirit of grace?"*

7. The covenant agreement is sealed with the communion supper. When we partake of it, we testify that we are part of the Body of

Christ and the Father's Kingdom. We are one with Him. In John 6:53 Jesus said, *"Most assuredly, I say to you, unless you eat the flesh of the Son of Man and drink His blood, you have no life in you."* By this covenant meal, God through Jesus Christ, guarantees us all His benefits as are outlined in His Word. As we approach the communion table, we are to realize that we have no righteousness within ourselves, but His death bought it. Your worthiness is a free gift from Jehovah through the power of the blood. When you take in the communion wine, you are literally taking God's life. This table is only for the saved so as not to cause the unsaved to be unworthy of it. The lost have no agreement with it. This blood represents everything that is good and wholesome, whole and holy. There is healing in the atonement.

8. An interminable memorial has been erected in the hearts of men forever. It is a tree framed as a cross, the symbol of our redemption. The Bible says in Galatians 3:13-14, *"Christ has redeemed us from the curse of the law, having become a curse for us (for it is written, 'Cursed is everyone who hangs on a tree'), that the blessing of Abraham might come upon the Gentiles in Christ Jesus, that we might receive the promise of the Spirit through faith."*

There should never be a thought of coming to the communion table to celebrate in our own righteousness, for if we do we receive it unworthily. You have been cleansed and robed in His righteousness. And, in fact, there is no scriptural reason for what is known as a closed communion. We are invited to the table to feast on His passion because we have missed the mark and have sinned and cannot cleanse ourselves. To disallow communion (for the redeemed), whether for yourself or others, is to say to God, "The sacrifice of Your Son was not enough to cleanse me from my sin. I must abstain from the table because I am guilty and unworthy."

This is the attitude toward closed communion. Someone other than God judges the worthiness of the offender. When this is said, you are actually saying to the Father, "Jesus' blood is not enough to redeem me. I know better than You! Therefore, I must stay away from the only sacrifice that can cleanse my sin until I deliver myself." This is all the same as saying you must save and sanctify yourself. You are on the verge of blasphemy of the Spirit.

God commands us as Christians to partake of the communion table and commends us when we do. We receive forgiveness and healing from all that afflicts or offends. Failure to recognize His Body simply means we have not discerned who the members are and all that His broken body purchased for us. **There is no greater or better covenant!** He has delivered you from inexorable death into eternal life. When this edict is broken, sickness may be the result and even physical death (1 Corinthians 11:23-34). We must confess to Him that we need Him in every aspect of our lives and we should commune with Him to celebrate our liberty and salvation regularly.

As we partake of His life, we become flesh of His flesh and bone of His bone. Salvation connotes that we have married the Lamb. A door has opened by which we may feel at one with God and interact with Him face to face. *"Therefore, brethren, having boldness to enter the Holiest by the blood of Jesus, by a new and living way which He consecrated for us, through the veil, that is, His flesh, and having a High Priest over the house of God, let us draw near with a true heart in full assurance of faith, having our hearts sprinkled from an evil conscience and our bodies washed with pure water"* (Hebrews 10:19-22). We may freely bring our requests to the Lord in the name of Jesus, for our covenant is authorized through Jesus' blood. If we sin He is quick to forgive. No requirement is necessary for another mediator. We have a High Priest and Mediator, Jesus Christ, who was bruised and pierced for us. When we hold out our hands to Him, He sees and entreats the Lord by presenting the issue of His own blood. No other provision will ever carry the same powers or capabilities.

Chapter 13

The Covenant of Christ

For God so loved the world that He gave His only begotten Son, that whoever believes in Him should not perish but have everlasting life. For God did not send His Son into the world to condemn the world, but that the world through Him might be saved.
John 3:16-17

There would be no reason to comprise a book on prophetic covenants were it not for the covenant that is the hallmark of all covenants, the covenant of Christ. It is a sad epitaph to Christianity that the major portion of Christians do not have a full understanding of their covenant and its rights, nor do they fully perceive what the totality of Christ's passion consists of.

The Prophet Isaiah aptly prophesied that a virgin would conceive and bear a Son (Isaiah 7:14). This divine child shall be called Emmanuel, or God now resides with us. He would eat butter and honey, to know to refuse what was evil and accept what is good. Butter and honey were representations of the good food of the land and would be a mainstay in a child's diet. This reference emphasized Jesus' humanity. The child would be great among His people and convert them to righteousness, restoring them to the Heavenly Father. Though the information seemed simplistic to the average hearer, it was a most difficult feat (though not impossible with God) to accomplish, considering the fact that it had to be done through and with sinful mankind.

Further revelation in the same chapter of Isaiah says that before the child can even know to eat butter and honey, Israel's foremost enemy of that hour would be defeated, but if they did not comply with faith, their enemies (the Assyrians) would defeat them.

They were told to be quiet and acquiescent and they would see the salvation of the Lord. If they did so, that land they dreaded would be forsaken of both of her kings. But as strong and prolific as the prophecy was, they did not mix the Word with faith and did not see its total fulfillment in Isaiah's day or in Christ's.

The Scripture says in Isaiah 7:21-22:

"It shall be in that day that a man will keep alive a young cow and two sheep; so it shall be, from the abundance of milk they give, that he will eat curds; for curds and honey everyone will eat who is left in the land."

Butter (curds) and honey were the mark of a land ravaged by the enemy. When all of the people were forced to eat this, it marked a land of sparse survivors and of ruined fields, orchards and desolate cities. This should have distinguished a time of awaiting the manifestation of the hand of deliverance of the Lord, for God desired to raise up deliverance for the house of David. The warning of trusting God by faith transcends time and space through millennia, foretelling the wasting of our covenant rights and powers if there is no trust in the Almighty. We who trust Him see the destruction of every false king. God did not allow the prophet's words to fall, for later the Prophet Micah confirmed Isaiah's prophecy to mankind by predicting the coming of the Savior to be born in Bethlehem, Judea. Now our land is not desolate; our covenant is intact.

Major Prophecies Fulfilled Concerning Christ

There are a plethora of scriptures that both prophesy the coming of Christ and define the Lord's intention. I shall briefly review several of the most dynamic of the predictive prophecies. The odds of all of these prophecies being fulfilled by one man range from multiplied millions to one. Genesis 3:15 tells us that the Seed of the woman will bruise the head of the serpent. Galatians 4:4 is its fulfillment, saying that in the fullness of time, God sent forth His Son born of a woman.

Genesis 12:3 says of Abram that God will bless those who bless him and curse those who curse him, and in him shall all the nations of the earth be blessed. Matthew 1:1 calls forth the genealogy of Christ, the Son of David, the Son of Abraham. Christ was the blessing of all generations, for salvation was retroactive toward those who died believing in the promise. This validates the importance of these early fathers who received the reassurance of salvation coming through their seed.

Numbers 24:17 finds the false prophet Balaam saying, *"A Star shall come out of Jacob; and a Scepter shall rise out of Israel.."* that will destroy the tyranny of the Moabites and the children of Sheth. Jacob is listed in the direct line of the Messiah. Isn't it a fascinating precept that God ordains prophets and they can do nothing except what He demands or allows, even sorcerers like Balaam! This false prophet accurately prophesied the coming of Christ.

Micah 5:2 declares Bethlehem Ephrathah, though small in deference to the cities of Israel, shall give birth to One who would be ruler in all Israel. Luke 2:27 says that Mary and Joseph were forced to go to their hometown to pay tribute, and she being great with child, was obliged to give birth to the Messiah in a stable in Bethlehem.

Isaiah 7:14 says that He will be born of a virgin. Luke 1:26-31 extols the coming of Gabriel the archangel to announce to a virgin named Mary the glad tidings of a Savior who would be born to her. Hosea 11:1 prophesies that, out of Egypt, God called His Son. This was a two-fold promise: Israel was redeemed from Egypt under Moses, and Mathew 2:14-15 tells us that Joseph fled with Mary and the baby into Egypt to avoid Herod's wrath that would have resulted in Christ's premature death. When the danger had passed, both parents and Jesus returned to Israel.

Malachi 3:1 predicts the messenger of the covenant (John the Baptist) shall prepare the way before the Lord. Luke 3 identifies him as John the Baptist. Jesus recognized John as the one who was to come before Him in the spirit of Elijah the prophet. John was considered the greatest prophet to live by Christ Himself.

Psalm 2:7 declares Him to be the Son of God. Luke 7:24 and John 1:34 also declare Him the Son of God. Isaiah 53:3 says that His own people would reject Him. John 1:11 says He came to His own but they did not receive Him. Psalm 41:9 foretold His betrayal at the hands of a friend. Luke 22:47-48 confirms Judas' perfidy against Christ with startling accuracy. In Zechariah 11:12 his price was weighed out for thirty pieces of silver. Matthew 26:15 concedes that the precise amount of thirty pieces of silver was given to Judas Iscariot for his treachery toward Christ.

Psalm 22:7 describes the tragedy of His being scorned and mocked. Luke 23:35 tells us that the soldiers and onlookers at Calvary asked mockingly, since He said He trusted in God, let God deliver Him if He is who God says He is. There were no bones broken (Psalm 34:20; John 19:32); His side was pierced (Zechariah 12:10; John 19:34); and He was buried with the rich (Isaiah 53:9; Matthew 27:57-60). His glorious resurrection and ascension were foretold in Psalms 16:10, 68:18 and Mark 16:6-7,19.

As you can see there are far too many infallible proofs to the fact that Jesus is the Messiah. The Bible says, *"In the mouth of ho or three witnesses shall every word be established"* (2 Corinthians 13:1 KJV). The Lord more than substantiated the legitimacy of His Son, making it virtually impossible to deny the authenticity of the Christian faith. That is why the apostle could so boldly say that man is without excuse for denying the existence of God and the need for a Savior in Romans 1:20: *"For since the creation of the world, His invisible attributes are clearly seen, being understood by the things that are made, even His eternal power and Godhead, so that they are without excuse."*

The Bible warns us, *"Without shedding of blood there is no remission [of sin]"* (Hebrews 9:22). Man's sin in Eden set the entire universe in disarray, causing all creation to groan to wit for the redemption of mankind. The blood of Jesus is the most powerful, valuable substance in the universe. It retroactively purchased the salvation of everyone who believed in He who was to come before His commitment was fulfilled as well as every future generation of believers. This miraculous, divine intervention took place in Heaven before the Word ever came to earth. God predicated this critical covenant's abilities upon His own spoken Word. Revelation 13:8 tells us that *"the Lamb [was] slain from the foundation of the world."* This substantiates the potent truth that the work was done before we drew breath.

The book of Hebrews gives us a more thorough understanding of the power of the covenant of Christ than perhaps any other book of the Bible. It traces the historical background of Jehovah's actions from the standpoint of the universal laws, to the law of Moses, onward to the law of redemption. Now because of Christ's sacrifice, we need only believe and receive instead of following the ordinances and rituals prescribed to obtain absolution. One valiant act of obedience was enough. However, it is not obedience for obedience sake, or that which any man could accomplish, but rather the One who was obedient that set the world aright.

Because of the lasting covenant, we have recognized certain ideals by which we live and believe in the Christian faith. The basic tenants of classical Christianity are:

God Almighty is the only God of the universe.

Christ Jesus was born of a virgin.

God robed Himself in sinful flesh.

God as Christ grew to full manhood and was tempted in all points as we are, yet did not sin.

The Father, Son and Spirit are one and uniquely manifest in three distinct personalities.

Christ was given a choice as to whether He would go to Calvary, and He conceded to the will of His Father.

His blood was spotless because He did not sin. Therefore, it being shed bought salvation and deliverance for all who would receive Him.

He was the only Man who could have redeemed mankind.

He died physically at Calvary, entered hell in our place, defeated Satan, and rose from the dead on the third day.

You must be born again to fully benefit from His redemptive work of salvation.

There is no other avenue to God or to Heaven but by the sacrifice of Christ.

We must be baptized in water as an act of strict obedience and contrition (not salvation).

As charismatic Christians, we add to this praiseworthy list the necessity for the baptism of the Holy Spirit for the upsurge of power in and for direction for our lives.

The Father, for our salvation and triumph, has provided everything necessary for our complete success in His Kingdom. We need only take advantage of these riches to obtain everlasting life and a good life with Him on earth as well as in Heaven. It is tragic to think that some, when offered the wonderful gift of His love, will reject it and destine themselves to a lifeless, hellish eternity.

The Ultimate Sacrifice: The Cross

All four of the gospels include a vivid adaptation of the sufferings of Christ at Calvary. It would be impossible for me to express the full portent of the pictures I have envisioned of this deplorable event, so forgive my inadequacies. I say deplorable with great caution of being misunderstood, for it was a most necessary event for our sakes. He took our death *in our place* causing us to be in His debt for all eternity, and then turning, cancelled our debt of sin by marking it paid in full, written in His own blood.

Just before His passion, Christ met with His disciples for the last time. He broke bread with them at the Passover feast and exposed His heart. Our Lord and blessed Savior took off His earthly apparel, girded Himself with a cloth and washed the feet of His disciples. Peter protested feeling much like most of us, so unworthy, and was chastised by Christ saying that if He could not wash Peter's feet, Peter could have no part in Him. Peter's response was, "Wash me all over." (That should be our response also. *Wash me thoroughly.*) He taught us through this action to wash each other's feet, and by doing this we would remain conscious of the fact that we are in this world for others and not just for ourselves. We should spread the love and humility of Christ to the entire world instead of the stench of religious hypocrisy.

After this, He regaled them with both ruminating and then gravely serious, ardent, veritable truths of life itself, finally concluding with the foreboding testimony of the duplicity by one who would "dip the sop" from His very bowl. Each disciple, according to the books of Matthew and Mark, dolefully inquired of

Him, "Is it I?" He adjured each of the faithful they were safe from being used to destroy Him and distinguished Judas Iscariot as the perpetrator. Immediately after the disclosure, Judas dips the sop, only to hear the Son inauspiciously speak: "What you must do, do quickly." He exits chillingly in pathos.

Christ retires with His disciples to the mountains to pray. He agonizes to the Father, imploring Him for another way to accomplish the same feat. Jesus willingly gave in to His Father's desire, and in the middle of His agony, returned to the camp and spoke to His followers, saying, *"My soul is exceedingly sorrowful, even to death. Stay here and watch with Me . . . What? Could you not watch with Me one hour? Watch and pray, lest you enter into temptation. The spirit indeed is willing, but the flesh is weak"* (Matthew 26:38, 40-41).

Watch that you enter not into temptation. This is a powerful warning for all who would live uprightly. Jesus is forced to awaken the once again slumbering disciples as the soldiers come to take Him away to be crucified. We are only too often slumbering disciples in the sight of the Lord when we should be awakened through prayer to both spiritual and natural events all around us.

Judas' kiss leaves its devastation upon His cheek; the soldiers seize Him; He is forced to perform a miracle for the sake of Peter's indignation; He is flogged with a cat-of-nine-tails mercilessly – all in an eternal moment of petrifying reality. Then begins the long trek forward up the Via Dolorosa. The weight of the cross overwhelmed our Messiah, buckling His legs and breaking the last of the strength of His human back. He falls and an unwitting spectator, a black man, Simon of Cyrene, carries it the remainder of the way. It has been "ours" to carry for this purpose to this very hour.

Spikes are execrably driven through His wrists (hands) and one single spike through each of His ankles pinning Him to the instrument of death. The agony is unbearable. As the cross is lifted *("And I, if I am lifted up from the earth, will draw all peoples to Myself." - John 12:32),* He cries out in excruciating pain. Two thieves converse with Him. One receives paradise, the other damnation; he condemned himself. When all this transpired He exclaimed, "I thirst." The attendant offered Him hyssop with myrrh, but when He had tasted it, He refused it. The hyssop was used in the original Passover to sprinkle the blood on the doorpost; the myrth was to deaden the pain. He refused it so that His pain would not be diminished one iota. He wanted to feel our pain when we are angst-ridden in life. Jesus' own mother's pain was so inconceivable, adding to His suffering. She had to be swiftly removed from the field. Our hearts can only imagine the heartache that ensued, for this mother pondered the salutations of the shepherds and angels at His birth.

For of a surety, you will never lead others where you yourself have not been or are unwilling to go. That is why Jesus is the Savior of the world, and we are told to take up our cross and follow Him. In the days in which we live, people often protest the showing or wearing of a crucifix, to which I reply, "If you have never seen Him on the cross, you will never see Him off of the cross!" The emblem serves as a true reminder of the pain and then impending joy of His death and resurrection. With every pulsating heartbeat the Father wept, the angels gazed transfixed, creation groaned; eternity stood in suspension.

Christ cried out with a loud voice, *"It is finished,"* and He bowed His head and died. Suddenly every unclean spirit in the universe went into rapturous revelry screaming with the atrociously evil principalities of darkness, "We've won. We've won!" as Jesus descended, barreling toward the unimaginable obscurity of hell. Satan came to mock Him, but was tormented by one solemn question that rang through the fathoms of hell: The Father asks with great fervor, "If you can find one single sin committed by this man, you have permission to keep Him here and rightfully take your place in

Heaven!" Satan of course could not, and Christ, empowered by the Holy Spirit, triumphantly demanded the keys to death, hell and the grave. *"Having disarmed principalities and powers, He made a public spectacle of them, triumphing over them in it"* (Colossians 2:15). **He** won; **we** won! He rose from death and "brought to pass the saying that is written: 'Death is swallowed up in victory" (1 Corinthians 15:54). The graves of those who died believing on the promise were opened and they were seen by over 500 witnesses. He's alive! Now the Father laughs and the people rejoice. He has risen just as He said He would!

Matthew says that Mary Magdalene, Mary His mother, and another woman went to the sepulchre to further embalm the body, when they were greeted by an angel who extolled them with the good news, *"He is not here; for He is risen, as He said. Come, see the place where the Lord lay"* (Matthew 28:6). John's account of the same incident is even more breathtaking. The women are greeted by a man dressed in white who is unrecognizable for a moment, until He calls one of them by name, Mary Magdalene. *"She turned and said to Him, 'Rabboni!' (which is to say, Teacher)"* (John 20:16). They were in a living ecstasy, the same as we should experience with the awesome first blush of salvation and wondrous anticipation of His love.

Now imagine the Father's joy as the Son ascends the first time carrying a basin of His own blood before the presence of the holy cherubim. He sprinkles it on the mercy seat of Heaven, the utensils of the altar and upon the record of our sins. In that moment, everyone who believed on Him and would believe in Him was saved for all eternity. Only then could He return and be touched by His disciples, particularly Thomas, the open skeptic (in reality they were all skeptical until they saw evidence of Him or, even better, saw Him. Thomas was bold enough to report his skepticism). The work was completed, the witness of His resurrection assured, the broken hearts mended. Now Jesus, the Christ ("Jehovah is salvation" with the implication of the future redemption), has become the Anointed One who has destroyed the yoke of bondage once and for all. We gladly rejoice.

> *Then the seventy returned with joy, saying, "Lord, even the demons are subject to us in Your name." And He said to them, "I saw Satan fall like lightning from heaven. "Behold, I give you the authority to trample on serpents and scorpions, and over all the power of the enemy, and nothing shall by any means hurt you. "Nevertheless do not rejoice in this, that the spirits are subject to you, but rather rejoice because your names are written in heaven." Luke 10:17-20*

Chapter 14
The Melchizedek Priesthood and The Covenant of Atonement

The book of Hebrews is a premiere book for outlining the covenant of Christ. It expresses the entirety of God's plan from the inauguration of the concept to its fruition. The opening salutation in Hebrews 1:1-2, declares, *"God, who at various times and in various ways spoke in time past to the fathers by the prophets, has in these last days spoken to us by His Son, whom He has appointed heir of all things, through whom also He made the worlds."* It further adjures us that we must not neglect so great a salvation. The Father solidifies the fact that He did not entrust the world to come into the hands of angels but placed all things under the feet of His Son.

The writer of Hebrews sets the order aright by giving surety to our authority as believers in Christ and His sacrifice, for in its pages we find that we the called are presented as "brethren," or in like disposition with Him. All rights and privileges accrued from being a member of God's family through Christ, are acknowledged in the statement, "I will declare your name to the brethren." Jesus' sufferings gave Him power over devils that is transferred to us by virtue of covenant. The Son of God is ascribed as the "High Priest of our confession," and we are admonished to receive this great salvation, for there is no other.

The most critical issues around which the book of Hebrews evolves are two-fold: (1) The ministry of Christ is superior to all that preceded it in the Old Covenant, and (2) Christ's priesthood is the ultimate priesthood and is not identified after Aaron but Melchizedek. In unfolding these issues the author dispenses the most acute reason for a lack of acceptance and growth in the understanding of the covenant described, and that is spiritual immaturity. This one major factor keeps the elders from being capable of instructing the flocks of God in the way of righteousness. Instead, it begets dullness of hearing, promotes the picking and choosing of what we will believe God has spoken and contemptuously destroys true discernment, among other things. It is a warning that has the ability to prevent neglect of God's Word, hardness of heart, unbelief, sinfulness and rebellion.

Jesus was to divorce the Aaronic priesthood in the truest sense and implement the kind of priesthood only defined by the life and ministry of Melchizedek. Melchizedek is defined as the king of Salem (i.e., Jerusalem) and as a priest of the Most High God, who went out to congratulate Abraham after his great victory over Chedorlaomer and his allies. He met Abraham in the valley of Shave (the valley of the kings). The priest bestowed blessings upon Abraham who gave a tithe of the spoil from the battle to him.

The Bible says that when this transpired, Levi was still in the loins of his father (giving credence to the fact that Levi, father of the priesthood, tithed to this great priest), but the tithe was considered in honor of the recognition of the royal priesthood of Melchizedek. It was not known at that point that God would call the priesthood out of Abraham. The tenth was, according to the general custom, the offering presented to the Lord. Melchizedek is mentioned in Psalm 110:4, where it is foretold that the Messiah would be *"a priest forever according to the order of Melchizedek,"* and in Hebrews 5:7, where these two passages of the Old Testament are quoted and the typical relationship between Melchizedek and our Lord is afforded an explanation of great length.

"According to the order of Melchizedek" is actually like saying, "In the same manner and official dignity as a king and priest." The mediator ministry of Christ, His role, function and responsibilities, is the likeness we are called to walk in as we advance in His very footsteps. Jesus was commanded to follow after the order of Melchizedek and for excellent reason. The Old Covenant separates prophet, priest and king, but Melchizedek was a composite of them all in one, an early form of a definition mirroring the apostolic of the New Covenant.

The relation between Melchizedek and Christ then, is set out in the following ways: Each was a priest (1) who is not of the Levitical tribe; (2) is superior to Abraham; (this is the theme of the book of Hebrews: Christ is superior to all that has gone on in the Old Covenant); (3) whose beginning and end are unknown; and (4) who is not only a priest, but also a king of righteousness and peace, and "who is without father or mother" (meaning one need not be born in a dynasty of ministers or even a Christian home, but our calling is assured because of His sacrifice). All that we need to fulfill our divine providence is provided if we pursue it through Christ, for because of Him we are now also priests forever (in His name) after the order of Melchizedek.

This beautifully divulged plan perfectly sets out for us the necessary factors in how to maximize our benefits from the greatest of all covenants, for the Testator of this Last Will and Testament died and returned to assure the implementation of His will. If we neglect this agreement, there is simply no other that may reconnect us to God. He is the only way. Now because of His priesthood, we can dare to enter the most holy place without fear as kings and priests. In this we can develop true faith, for we have Someone by whom to pattern our faith and trust. We are strengthened by His words to us and can run the race patiently realizing that the same Jesus who started us on the journey will complete it in us. Hebrews 8:1 sums up the matter of the Melchizedek priesthood. It says:

"Now this is the main point of the things we are saying:
We have such a High Priest, who is seated at the right hand of the throne of the Majesty in the heavens, a Minister of the

sanctuary and of the true tabernacle which the Lord erected, and not man."

Covenant and the Atonement

The renowned story of the exodus from Egypt to Israel, the land of the promise, set the criterion upon which we developed the practice of communion. Israel's deliverance from bondage and re-acceptance of Jehovah was consummated in this festival of consecration to God. Many Christians have mistakenly believed that Jesus first instigated communion on the night in which He was betrayed, but communion stemmed from the Passover. Moses, Israel's heroic leader, was sent to Ramses, Pharaoh of Egypt, to relay a message from heaven: *"Let My people go!"* According to the book of Exodus, Pharaoh refused the command, causing the Lord to resort to extreme measures. God disturbed Egypt with intense plagues, the final judgment culminating in the reason for the Passover.

Moses warned that if the children of Israel were not released from Egypt, God Almighty would relinquish the angel of death to bring a horrid verdict upon the firstborn of every household, including Pharaoh's. The Bible states that God had hardened Pharaoh's heart and he would not obey. The terminology implies that the Lord placed this obstinacy within the man's heart, but this is not a literal. Covenant dictates that its rule circumvents all others. The Word is the law of God's covenant and if you come against it, you will reap the consequences. Grave misunderstandings have been propagated by the fact that humans, particularly religious ones, do not seem to comprehend the power of authorities under a covenant rule.

Moses was a pre-New Testament apostle with all rights and privileges of that office. When he spoke, he spoke directly for God and His Kingdom. To deny Moses was the same as denying God. When a prophet or apostle speaks as God even today, that authority still is enforced from Heaven. Even though it carries an enormous amount of responsibility, God still dispenses it through individuals He has ordained to the higher offices. Penalties may ensue from mild to extreme in consequence. Pharaoh's consequence of coming up against "heavens of brass" due to his rebellion, was to have his sin to harden his heart against the laws of God.

The Latin word for this kind of delegated authority enjoyed by Moses and others is plenipotentiary. It is defined as a surrogate official representing a king, with commissioned orders assigned delegating to that officer the same rights and privileges given the potentate (supreme ruler), only void of the superior's throne, possessions and far reaching, assiduous scope of authority. To follow the plenipotentiary is the same as following the orders of the potentate. To defy him is to defy the One who sent him.

Christianity has seriously watered down this concept, dictating that all people are equal in the sight of God and have equal authority. While the first premise is an absolute truth, the second could not be further from the truth! Two important qualities define a kingdom: officers and authorities, and laws and bylaws. When an authority is functioning under his full mantle, he is to be reverenced, for his power comes from God. Therefore, Pharaoh suffered great loss for resisting Moses' preeminence. The same may happen today if the infraction occurs against God's holy assigns. Once again, it is not resisting a personality that is the offence but resistance to God's rule.

In the case of the institution of Passover, God ordained this celebration because of the callousness of Egypt's leaders. Israel understands the true meaning of liberation because she was forced to cry out from the disparaging brickyards. Despite the fact that Israel attempted to fit into the surrounding civilization to the point of worshipping their idolatrous deities, God's faithfulness prevailed for the sake of His anointed. Egypt did not realize how God had visited them and persecuted His visitation after the death of Joseph. Moses was raised up in that empire and knew its customs well. He had in-house training advantage. When it became necessary to do the will of God, Moses had already spent eighty years going through the process. They could despise his anointing, but they could not refute or diminish his power. He was the plenipotentiary.

When God speaks through the assigned apostle or prophet, the officer is most potent in his sphere of domain. For Moses it was the country of his birth as well as the place of his inheritance. Each plague (as covered earlier) attacked and devastated an Egyptian deity. The last and final plague conquered a long-standing principality. In Eden, Satan seduced the first Adam (male and female). Passover was a type and shadow of the triumph of the second Adam. God's first "created" son, Adam, fell prey to the seduction. His fall caused death to reign even to the extent that the firstborn son of Adam and Eve became a murderer. Jehovah knew that He had to initiate a spiritual precedent that would reach so far into the future it would retroactively shine back upon man reflecting the face of the Messiah.

That reflection was in the blood of the Passover. On that night they were instructed to roast a lamb whole and eat all but its waste parts. They were to eat bitter herbs with the roasted lamb and unleavened bread. Each food represented a prophetically simulated message from the Lord. The bitter herbs reminded them of the pain of the brickyards, the lamb represented the Messiah who would be slain wholly and completely for their sakes, etc. The unleavened bread called *"the bread of affliction"* (Deuteronomy 16:3) reminded them of their past affliction, and symbolized the new life cleansed from the leaven of malice and wickedness of the old Egyptian lifestyle.

Leaven was forbidden in all offerings (Leviticus 2:4-5), because it stood for the hypocrisy and misleading doctrines of the flesh immersed in sin. The scripture says in First Corinthians 5:7-8,

"Therefore purge out the old leaven, that you may be a new lump, since you truly are unleavened. For indeed Christ, our Passover, was sacrificed for us. Therefore let us keep the feast, not with old leaven, nor with the leaven of malice and wickedness, but with the unleavened bread of sincerity and truth."

The Symbols of Passover and Jesus' Passion

The twelfth chapter of the book of Exodus gives the procedure for the Passover celebration. In that same chapter the Lord gives them the directives for the celebration of the Passover after the exodus. The Lord prescribed seven days of feasting, referring to it as the feast of unleavened bread. They were to roast the lamb after draining its blood in a basin. They were to choose it on the tenth day and slay it on the fourteenth day. The blood was to be smeared on the doorpost with hyssop on the side lintels, top and bottom.

Initially they were told to eat all of the lamb and destroy what was left over. They were to eat it with their shoes and clothing on, ready to depart at any moment. The feast had to take place at night. At about midnight the death angel by the hand of the Lord executed the last and final plague that procured the freedom of the Jews. The firstborn sons of Egypt perished, while those of Israel were spared. Wherever the blood was applied, the angel passed over the dwelling. An astonishing set of comparisons can be made to the original Passover and the sacrifice of Christ. On the tenth day of the month Abib the lamb was chosen and sacrificed on the fourteenth day. On the tenth day of the same month Jesus made His triumphal entry into Jerusalem to celebrate the feast of the Passover. On the fourteenth day He was condemned to die.

The lamb's throat was cut at precisely 3:00 p.m. (the ninth hour) after which the blood was placed on the doorposts. Jesus was crucified at the sixth hour, cried out with a loud voice in the ninth hour and gave up the ghost. The priest was cutting the throat of the lamb in the sign of the cross at the same time. The lamb was roasted whole with its entrails wrapped about the head so as not to permit the entrails with the waste within to be roasted in the body. It would contaminate the lamb. None of its bones were broken. Jesus paralleled the lamb in that He totally embraced this holocaust of suffering. His blood flowed from His hands, feet and head, marking the four points the blood was smeared on the doorposts and lintels. He wore a crown of thorns upon His head. Not one of His bones was broken.

The lamb's flesh was distributed among the participants and consumed. Jesus is the bread of life, and whenever we receive communion we commemorate His death. We are told by Him to eat His flesh and drink His blood, to eat and drink all of it. The wine was for cleansing and purification. We are told by the Apostle Paul to examine ourselves so as not to take the wine unworthily. Fire sanctifies and Christ sanctified us through the fires of His affliction, just as the original lamb was roasted by fire. During the Passover the firstborn sons of Egypt were killed because of Pharaoh's disobedience. Christ, the last Adam, was the firstborn Son of God who was sacrificed for all sinful sons to bring life to all who receive Him.

The lamb was sacrificed for the atonement from sin for the Israelites during the Passover. Sin caused the death angel to be released to take the lives of the firstborn sons of Egypt. The blood of a lamb kept the firstborn sons of Israel alive. Jesus' atonement during the Passover celebration caused His blood first to be splattered in His scourging in the courts of His enemies, and then along the Via Dolorosa (the way of suffering) all the way to being nailed to the cross. His blood fell to the ground on the way to Calvary in front of the very temple sight before which He observed the blood of the lamb(s) flowing down the temple mount. The blood of Jesus cleanses from all unrighteousness, and mercy caused the blood of the Savior to save the lives of all who would believe.

After the Passover, a two-day journey into the wilderness brought the children of the promise to the Red Sea. The second night all through the night, they miraculously crossed over on dry ground arriving in safety on the third day. Their enemies were drowned in the sea. Prior to His passion, Jesus had several experiences of note on the sea, foremost among them being the fact that this vehicle of sudden death (a stormy sea) was so conquered by Him He walked upon it! Jesus also walked through the valley of death while in the grave for two days and was raised to life on the third day.

Joseph's bones were carried from Egypt to the promised land for burial, leaving his former tomb empty. He was laid to rest in the long-awaited land of paradise that he would never see again. Jesus causes us to boast of His empty tomb, for He was raised from the dead to restore us to the paradise of God that we have never seen. The entire process was completed in just seven days (God's number of completion), but its effects will last for all eternity. Isaiah 53 distinguishes each step in the process and what it accomplished. He began by asking who received the report of the events that secured our salvation and to whom did God reveal Himself?

Jesus would grow up as a vulnerable, tender child in a seemingly barren place, and as an adult He would not be extremely handsome that one might be drawn to Him. He would endure grave persecution and rejection. People would shrink back at His goodness and hide. He bore our griefs and carried our sorrows to the cross, yet we considered His suffering as being issued punitively by God. All of us have gone off course and God placed upon Him our wickedness. His bruises and whiplashes took on the burdensome scourging of sin and the ravaging of sickness, resulting in our healing.
God was content (figuratively) with His being bruised because we were the prizes. He did not complain or cry by virtue of His suffering, and as a sheep is led to the slaughter, He dutifully followed His course. He was buried in a rich man's grave, and who shall declare His generations?

Chapter 15

The Genealogy of Christ

The book of the genealogy of Jesus Christ, the Son of David, the Son of Abraham. Matthew 1:1

The book of Matthew in the first chapter gives the genealogy of Jesus Christ from His earthly father's lineage. A similar genealogy is found in the third chapter of the book of Luke. Some might pose the argument, why Joseph's line and not Mary's, considering the fact that Jesus was not born as an issue of Joseph and Mary's copulation. Some scholars consider that the genealogy listed in Luke's gospel is actually Mary's and not Joseph's, that Joseph is mentioned because he is Mary's husband and Jesus' earthly father. The genealogy of Luke covers the lineage from the standpoint of the natural line of descendants as opposed to Matthew covering the royal line.

Needless to say, whatever is true, both lineages are justified in being recorded, for the history of Christ's family shows how we can qualify as being kings and priests underneath the King and High Priest of our calling, for we are royalty out of a common lineage, just like Melchizedek. Women were considered very significant in the eyes of God, as is surmised by the naming of particular women among the forebearers of Jesus through Joseph. However, because women do not possess seed they are not considered the critical element in the naming or perpetuity of a lineage. Interestingly enough, no women are mentioned in Luke's rendition of the family tree of Christ for the reason just stated. Women are incubators who receive and produce the children coming from the loins of the male, but cannot reproduce in and of themselves. This is why she vitally completes the male and rewards him with reproducing himself through her in the earth, a major key to understanding God's plan.

Just as important is the fact that woman came out of man and in this, we bow to the Lord for His wisdom in so doing. Therefore, no woman should feel slighted or left out because both genealogies reflect from Joseph to Adam, or vice versa, with the emphasis on the male. The man was also the first created, which was God's way of enjoining and substantiating the factor of the woman's genesis beginning in him. Therefore, if he is named covenantally, so is she.

Jehovah showed the necessity of earthly fathers in the lives of their children. He could have sent Jesus to a single parent home but did not, for the shaping of the spirit of the child is done by the father, in conjunction with the mother, who was charged by God to raise the children to know the Lord. This was to be an example for all households as to the perfect will of God concerning both the family and His Church.

In the list of descendants outlined in Matthew, chapter 1, we find every race, every kindred and every tongue represented. Each strata and sphere of society, along with all types of the human experience, are exemplified in the genealogy. Every name mentioned is Jewish (either by birth or by becoming proselytes), which signifies Judaism being a religion and not a race. Because Jews intermarried with other Jews so as not to be unequally yoked or tempted to whore after other gods, what may be distinguished as racial characteristics began to show themselves. The Lord is making a declaration that we as Christians and Jews are family coming from the same line enjoying the same kinds of human experiences. All of this is covered by the characters named in this list, and the divine intervention of the cleansing blood of Jesus. He brings deliverance from everything that could possibly plague humanity.

The descendants of Shem eventually settled in the colder regions and became the fairer in complexion, the Caananites came out of Ham who was Black, those who became Asian are represented between Abraham and David, and lastly, those considered red are a combination of Black, the compound that created the Asians, and white, all of them being reflected in this lineage. David represented the ultimate kingly and priestly anointing; Rahab was a woman of ill repute, representing the debased sinner; Tamar represented the disenfranchised who are given a pledge, denied it, but then fulfilled in God; Mary represented the pure who awaited the promise; and all of them represent family which is the relational presentation of Christ to the Church, His wife. Now you will hopefully understand the enormous purpose in recording the genealogies.

Matthew's genealogy is broken up into fourteen generational segments: from David to Moses, from Moses to the Babylonian captivity, from the Babylonian captivity to Christ. If a conscientious observer were to count the generations from Babylon to Christ, he would find only thirteen listed. Matthew 1:12-16 says:

And after they were brought to Babylon, Jeconiah begot (1) Shealtiel, and Shealtiel begot (2) Zerubbabel. Zerubbabel begot (3) Abiud, Abiud begot (4) Eliakim, and Eliakim begot (5) Azor. Azor begot (6) Zadok, Zadok begot (7) Achim, and Achim begot (8) Eliud. Eliud begot (9) Eleazar, Eleazar begot (10) Matthan, and Matthan begot (11) Jacob. And Jacob begot (12) Joseph the husband of Mary, of whom was born (13) Jesus who is called Christ.

Was there a mistake on the part of the writer, the genealogist, or perhaps the translators or scribes? In order to answer that question, we must once again take a look at Isaiah, chapter 53. At the conclusion of the chapter of this book titled, "The Covenant of Christ," a brief synopsis of Isaiah 53 is recorded. In a single chapter, the entirety of His life and commitment is prolifically assayed. Prior to our examination of Isaiah, we will take a look at the crucifixion through the eyes of John and David.

The Psalmist David graphically shows us His crucifixion in Psalm 22. He begins with the plaintiff salutation, *"My God, My God, why have You forsaken Me?" You can clearly hear the Father being implored as to why He is so far from His Son. The soldiers echoed*

David's declaration, "He trusted in the Lord ... let Him deliver Him since He delights in Him!" (V. 8). The psalmist professes, "They trusted, and You delivered them" (V. 4). This is an interesting symmetry, considering the fact that the psalmist spoke both for the people who trust in God and the Christ who would give Himself for a ransom.

The bulls of Bashan encompass Him, a description of the demonic presence represented on the hill that day. He is described as being poured out like water. His joints are pulled apart without a bone being broken. The hands and feet are pierced, and lots are cast for His garment. John 19:28 says, *"After this, Jesus, knowing that all things were now accomplished, that the Scripture might be fulfilled, said, 'I thirst!'"* and the psalmist proclaims, *"My tongue clings to My jaws ..."* (Psalm 22:15).

The book of John's elucidatory narrative wrenches our hearts with the horrors of His flogging, the pain of the weight of the cross as He walked the Via Dolorosa, the agony of those who loved Him who watched helplessly, the excruciating ache of the nails driven through flesh, the pathos and mock horror of His mother's grief, the indifference of the soldiers, all within a few short hours of eternity. The terror of those moments would be impossible for the greatest writers to depict entirely. We may only vicariously experience them through our love and His Spirit. All of this was done for the sake of love. Love found a way to bring redemption.

David's psalm ends victoriously, asserting:
"A posterity shall serve Him. It will be recounted of the Lord to the next generation, They will come and declare His righteousness to a people who will be born, that He has done this." Psalm 22:30-31

This perfectly correlates with our focus upon Isaiah 53:10-11, which says:

"Yet it pleased the Lord to bruise Him; He has put Him to grief. When You make His soul an offering for sin, He shall see His seed, He shall prolong His days, and the pleasure of the Lord shall prosper in His hand. He shall see the labor of His soul, and be satisfied. By His knowledge My righteous Servant shall justify many, for He shall bear their iniquities."

"He shall see His seed" after all that was declared has transpired. How can this be considering the fact that Jesus never married nor sired a child? The key is in His being made an offering for sin – the key is the cross!

We counted in Matthew's last group of fourteen generations only thirteen fathers including Christ, but the author did not make an error. In actuality there were far more than fourteen generations in each increment, but those through whom God brought certain deliverance or with whom marked history was made, there were recorded fourteen per increment in Heaven. When each of these forefathers and mothers walked through their adversities and triumphs, *Christ was in them*, but when He went to the cross in their place, *they were in Christ!* As He walked the way of suffering, we were in Him. As He endured the torment of the enemies that flogged Him, we were in Him. When He hung between here and eternity laden with our sin, sickness and disease, we were in Him. When He died and went to hell, we were in Him, and when He rose triumphant from the grave bearing the keys to death, hell and the grave, *we were in Him!*

Jesus' side was pierced just after His death. Blood and water gushed forth, proving that death's icy clasp had surely swallowed Him. That is what makes His resurrection even more potent. He bore our iniquity, as a mother would carry a child in her womb. It is said that in the Aramaic, the Hebrew words for *"Why have You forsaken me?"* could have been translated, *"For this reason came I into the world."* Christ came into the world to condemn sin and save the people of the world. He unreservedly succeeded, making a way for all men to receive this precious, necessary gift from the Father.

God opened the side of the first Adam to remove a single piece from which the man's wife was sculpted. *Men* opened the side of the last Adam so that Christ's death might give birth to His bride; she was born in the bloody flux (unrest or turbulence) of adversity and Calvary. Like the first Adam, the last Adam had to be put to sleep in death in order to bring life to His wife. The Bible says through the Prophet Isaiah, *"He shall see His seed, He shall prolong His days"* (v. 10). Though He had no children by natural means, that day He begot multiplied billions of children by the Spirit. His suffering that sent Him into the sleep of death for our sakes was as the labor pains that birthed a new era for the Kingdom of God. He bridged the Testaments, even causing time to stand still and then be revised. Jesus is the only Man who knows the labor pains of birth in that manner, for He has seen His seed and prolonged His days on the earth. If you are born again, your sin is pardoned by and through His blood. This enables you to say beyond a doubt that Jesus did not die barren; you are His seed, for **we** are the fourteenth generation of Christ.

Bibliography

The International Standard Bible Encyclopedia (Electronic Database by Biblesoft, 1996).

Nelson's Illustrated Bible Dictionary (Thomas Nelson, Publishers, 1986).

The New Exhaustive Strong's Numbers and Concordance with Expanded Greek-Hebrew Dictionary (Biblesoft and International Bible Translators, Inc., 1994).

The New Unger's Bible Dictionary (Chicago, IL: Moody Press, 1988).

The Online Bible, Thayer's Greek Lexicon and Brown, Driver & Briggs Hebrew Lexicon (Canada, Ontario: Woodside Bible Fellowship, 1993).

About the Author

Pamela Marion Green Vinnett, author of This Psychic Prophetic Age, For Women Only and co-author of Let the Prophets Speak, is the middle child of three children born to William and the late Dorothy Wigfall Green of Youngstown, Ohio. Both parents being professionals (her father an attorney and her mother a classical vocal concert artist), they demanded the very best of their children and groomed them for excellence in every undertaking.

The author's formal education reaches toward a Master's of Fine Arts degree, with an obtained Bachelor of Fine Arts in Vocal Performance with a double minor in Piano and Instrumentation, plus World History. Her vocal career is quite accomplished, having mastered, studied and performed more than nineteen operatic roles throughout the Eastern United States and parts of Europe, winning many prestigious vocal awards, including the Cleveland District Metropolitan Opera.

In later years, while working for the Cincinnati Opera Company, Pamela received Jesus as her personal Lord and Savior. That same year she was filled with the Holy Spirit and called into the ministry. Her life took a radical change that eventually led to the apostolic/prophetic ministry she now functions in today.

In 1983 Pamela Green married entrepreneur and businessman, George Vinnett, of St. Rose, Louisiana, and soon after began a journey of world-traveling itinerant ministry.

Pamela recognizes the cry of God's heart in this hour for integrity, sincerity, consistency and faithfulness to God in Christ. With a tremendously consuming mandate from God to assist in the reconstruction of His Kingdom, she is reaffirming the office of the apostle and the prophet, which will allow the Church to function to its fullest authority and level of proficiency.

Pamela is a profound author, instructor, and minister who has become a premier voice in the apostolic and prophetic movement. She is a mentor and spiritual mother to many, laying the foundation concerning the ministries of the apostle and the prophet to the latter day church and beyond.

Apostle Vinnett's career in ministry now spans over four decades. She has delivered the word of the Lord to seated presidents and kings, governors, senators, CEOs of corporations, and many of the most powerful Christian and secular leaders in the world, as well as individuals, churches, organizations, and nations. As an instructor she has taught on Kingdom principles, apostolic doctrine, and prophetic protocol in many prestigious institutions of higher learning, including Oral Roberts University and her own school of the prophetic. She is the founder of Pam Vinnett Ministries, Apostolic Initiatives In Motion (AAIM) Fellowship, and God's Apostolic Training Embassy (GATE) Fellowship, and is also chairman of Kingdom International Assemblies (KIA) Fellowship, headed by Apostle Rick Daniels of Florida, where she is principally submitted.

www.ingramcontent.com/pod-product-compliance
Lightning Source LLC
Chambersburg PA
CBHW071929290426
44110CB00013B/1536